What Happens Sunday Morning

What Happens Sunday Morning

*A Layperson's Guide
to Worship*

Carol M. Norén

Westminster/John Knox Press
Louisville, Kentucky

Scripture quotations from the New Revised Standard Version of the Bible are copyright © 1989 by the Division of Christian Education of the National Council of the Churches of Christ in the U.S.A., and are used by permission.

Book design by Kristen Dietrich

First edition

Published by Westminster/John Knox Press
Louisville, Kentucky

This book is printed on acid-free paper that meets the American National Standards Institute Z39.48 standard.

PRINTED IN THE UNITED STATES OF AMERICA
9 8 7 6 5 4 3 2 1

Library of Congress Cataloging-in-Publication Data

Norén, Carol Marie
    What happens Sunday morning : a layperson's guide to worship /
Carol M. Norén — 1st ed.
            p.   cm.
    Includes bibliographical references.
    ISBN 0-664-25227-3
    1. Public worship.   I. Title.
BV15.N67 1992
264—dc20   91–20973

To David Noren

a faithful layman

Contents

Introduction

On any Sunday millions of people in the United States will attend a Christian service of worship. It is this event that brings the largest number of church members together at the same time in the same place. Those attending will follow some form of liturgy, sing, hear a portion of the scriptures read, perhaps listen to an anthem by the choir, and hear a sermon preached by a minister. On some occasions they will participate in the Lord's Supper, or Eucharist. When the service is over, the worshipers are likely to have definite opinions about whether or not the service reflected, strengthened, and proclaimed their faith in Jesus Christ.

This book is based on three premises. The first is that despite regular church attendance, many lay people are unclear about what is supposed to happen in a service of worship. The second is that worshipers in a congregation are not simply observers. The third is that a greater understanding of what goes on in a service will enable worshipers to be participants and thus have a more significant worship experience.

Lack of clarity about what is supposed to happen in worship often results from the absence of criteria for understanding and appreciating worship. In the chapters that follow, some basic criteria are suggested, and readers are directed, when needed, to other resources from their own denomination. When people in the church study this material as a group, they will likely experience considerable agreement about the criteria for "good" worship. This agreement will enhance congregational unity. Worshipers are more likely after using this book to be active participants in worship, and their participation will in turn provide clearer and more constructive feedback for the pastor who has responsibility for planning and leading the service. Everyone's satisfaction with the worship service is likely to be greater when issues of understanding and participation are addressed by a class, a committee, or an entire congregation.

Each chapter will deal with one of six aspects of Christian worship: worship, the role of the laity, the physical setting, the music, the sermon, and the liturgy. Each chapter will include a discussion of the subject at hand and a series of questions that will enable individuals to react to the practice in their church and to compare their reactions with those of others using this book.

This guide is designed for use by groups in local churches such as worship committees and church school classes. If you have not talked much with others in the past about worship and your faith, you may be tempted to work through the book alone. Please resist that temptation! Because what happens on Sunday morning is a corporate activity, this guide will be of most benefit if several people in the church read and discuss it together. To borrow a phrase from Ecclesiastes 4:9, "Two are better than one, because they have a good reward for their toil." In this case, the "reward" is a better worship ministry.

What kind of group can use this book? If your church has a worship committee or other planning body, that may be the ideal group. An altar guild, weekday social/service/study group, or adult church school class can also benefit from working through the chapters together. Any ad hoc group of lay people in the church who are interested in worship may decide to use this guide. It is hoped that persons will read the first part of each chapter and then attend a worship service together in their church. They should not try to answer the questions at the end of each section until after the worship service, at their next meeting. Then they may compare their responses and discuss some or all of the following:

1. How does this aspect of our worship compare with what we read in the book?

2. Do our answers to the questions suggest change is needed?
3. What specific things can we do to bring about the desired changes?
4. How will we determine if the change has been a wise one?

By using this book, church members will not only achieve a better understanding of their service of worship but they also will be better able to evaluate and plan what happens on Sunday morning.

Many persons have helped me in the development of material for this book. My thanks to the late Robert L. Wilson, Professor of Church and Society at Duke Divinity School, who had the idea for the project and who assisted in several chapters and the formulation of discussion questions; Dean Dennis Campbell and Professors Teresa Berger and Richard Lischer, of The Duke Divinity School, who made helpful suggestions after reading parts of the manuscript; Mel and Marilyn Franklin, church members who kept me in touch with the layperson's point of view; the faithful congregations of Salem United Methodist Church in Barrington, Illinois, and Gorton Methodist and Trinity Ancoats Methodist Churches in Manchester, England. Finally, appreciation is also due Ginny W. Ashmore and Wanda D. Dunn for typing and retyping the manuscript.

C.M.N.

1. Why We Are Here

If you have a God, you must of necessity worship Him.
—Martin Luther

A worship committee wanted to improve the quality of their church's worship services and to increase attendance, so they conducted a survey of the members asking why they came to worship. Not surprisingly, they found that people attended the church for a wide variety of reasons. Some of the reasons given included:

— I come to worship to get my "batteries recharged" by a good sermon.
— All my friends are here.
— I've always gone to church.
— It's about the only thing we do together as a family.
— The Bible says you're supposed to go to church.
— I make sure I'm there whenever they have the Lord's Supper.
— I want to sing familiar hymns and hear a sermon that speaks to my needs.
— I need to know more about God, and God seems so close when I'm here.
— My parents/husband/wife make(s) me come.
— It's the smart thing to do (this person's employer was a member of the same church).
— I want my children to grow up in the church.
— I love the music.

Some of these answers may impress you as being more valid than others. Place a check next to the answers with which you agree. As you think about the reasons for your

choices, you will find your own theology of worship beginning to emerge. Expand the list to include other reasons you
know people have for attending worship. Place a check next
to these additional reasons with which you agree.

Theology of Worship

A theology of worship is a person's or a church's understanding of what Christian worship means and why it is conducted as it is. You probably have never asked yourself,
"What is my theology of worship?" That does not mean you
do not have one, nor that it has not changed as you have
grown and matured. A church's theology of worship is the
foundation for the decisions made concerning what happens
on Sunday morning. It draws upon understanding of the
Bible, knowledge of the church's history, the memory of
what has been done in the past, a sense of what is true and
right and reasonable, and what is meaningful to the individual or community at worship. In some denominations, particularly those such as Lutheran, Presbyterian, Episcopalian,
and United Methodist that have a central authority, the denomination's history and standards of worship practice are
also factors in determining a theology of worship.

People and churches may disagree about what worship is
and how it should be conducted. When they do, feelings can
be intense. Congregations may split and go their separate
ways. This does not necessarily mean that those who disagree are narrow-minded, stubborn, or not really Christian.
More likely, splits occur because a discussion of the meaning
of worship puts people in touch with ultimate values, those
beliefs that they consider of utmost importance. This is
ground no one should surrender lightly.

For example, a staunch church member was deeply troubled when the new pastor had a college student assist in
serving Holy Communion to the congregation. This person
did not cause a scene but telephoned a friend who was a
minister to ask if this incident was as bad as she thought.
The conversation revealed that her misgivings could be
traced back to her understanding of the theology of worship.

Her knowledge of what the Bible said about the Lord's Supper was limited to the Gospel narratives and the portions of 1 Corinthians that are included in most traditions' Words of Institution. These words were sacred to her, to be spoken reverently by a particular person during the service. Their solemnity was threatened by the presence of an unfamiliar and nonordained person in that part of worship.

She had little knowledge of church history, but she remembered that in her denomination not just anyone could preach or celebrate the sacraments. In her congregation, no college student had ever served communion. If anyone assisted the minister, it was a member of the official board. This was a special honor and responsibility for persons who had been elected by the congregation. The incident with the college student violated local custom and the values attached to it. At the same time, the church member realized that a new minister would not do things exactly the same way the former one had done and that the college student had acted as reverently as the board members would have. Finally, she knew she was among many who were put off by the casual, almost offhand way the new pastor led the rest of worship. She missed the reverence and mystery that worship services used to have. The real difficulty, she concluded, was not with the college student per se but with conflicting expectations of what a service of Holy Communion should be. She could now talk about *her* theology of worship as opposed to that of her pastor.

Do Christians have the right to say there are "bad" theologies of worship? Inadequate, myopic, or unorthodox might be better terms than "bad." A Christian theology of worship cannot deliberately ignore certain important matters. These include:

— what the Bible says;
— what the church has done through the ages;
— what denominational and local practices have been;
— why such practices have been followed;
— what is right and reasonable; and
— what has meaning in the worship experience of the individual or congregation.

Without getting into specific questions of how one denomination's worship practices differ from another's, consider some ways in which an authentic Christian theology of worship may be modeled in your local congregation.

Biblical Foundations for Christian Worship

First, worship looks to the Bible for guidance, especially the way the followers of Jesus worshiped. The early Christians gathered on the first day of the week (Sunday). They did so not only because this was the day of their Lord's resurrection but also not to interfere with their participation in synagogue services. The apostles were Jews who took seriously God's commandment to "remember the Sabbath day, to keep it holy."

From reading the Book of Acts and some of Paul's letters, we know that early Christian worship was based on things Jesus taught his followers to do:

1. They "came apart" to pray (see Luke 11:1–4; Acts 2:1–21; Acts 12:12; 1 Thess. 5:16, 17). Often, when we think about preaching and conversion in the early church, we are reminded of open-air, missionary messages such as the one Peter preached on the day of Pentecost or Paul's sermon at Mars Hill. The importance of this public witness cannot be overestimated, but followers of Jesus also met in members' homes or went elsewhere to meet in "closed session." Here they would pray, teach, admonish, and encourage each other in the Christian faith. People were gathered in Jesus' name for a common purpose: to praise God.

2. They read the scriptures (the Old Testament plus letters and Gospels to which they had access), taught, and preached (Luke 4:16–22; Luke 7:24–35; Acts 13:4, 5; 2 Timothy 4:2 and elsewhere). This was an aspect of worship they inherited from the synagogue. The Jewish custom was to use a rotating lectionary or calendar of readings in worship. After a lesson was read aloud by an appointed person, the rabbi would interpret and comment on it. In addition to this, psalms were sung or prayed, and one portion of scripture might be used to interpret or illuminate

another. An example of this is found in Jesus' pronounce-
ments that begin "You have heard it said of old . . . but I
say to you . . ." and in his reading and exposition of the
prophet Isaiah, recorded in Luke 4. The style of preaching
or teaching based on scripture varied—as is evident when
we compare the preaching of, for example, Peter, Paul,
and Stephen—but all are consistent in the high authority
attributed to God's Word and the belief that this Word
testifies to the lordship of Jesus Christ.

3. They baptized in the name of the Father, the Son, and the
Holy Spirit (see Matt. 28:19; Acts 19:1–7). Before Jesus
gave the Great Commission, John the Baptist had been
administering a baptism of repentance—not the same as
Christian baptism. Jesus commanded his followers to
baptize in the threefold name. This baptism, plus belief in
the crucified and risen Christ as Son of God, was what set
Christians apart from other religious people.

4. They exercised spiritual gifts (see Luke 10:17; Acts 2:1–4; 1
Corinthians 12:1–11; James 5:13–18). Individual persons
sometimes received special spiritual gifts during Jesus'
earthly ministry; for example, he sent out the Seventy and
gave them power to preach, to heal, and to cast out
demons. As a church, however, followers first received and
exercised spiritual gifts on the day of Pentecost when the
Holy Spirit came upon the disciples. The gifts of the Spirit
manifested during worship included the utterance of wisdom; knowledge; faith; healing; miracle working;
prophecy; discernment between spirits; speaking in
tongues, and interpretation of tongues. In writing to the
Corinthian congregation, Paul expressed concern about the
orderly and gracious exercising of these gifts and said the
greatest manifestation of the Holy Spirit among Christians
at worship was love. The early church believed the purpose
of these gifts was to glorify God, bear witness that Jesus
was the Messiah, and build up the fellowship of believers.

5. They celebrated a meal we have come to call the Eucharist,
or Holy Communion (see 1 Cor. 11:23–32; Jude 12; 2 Peter
2:13). "Eucharist" comes from the Greek word *eucharistia*,
or thanksgiving. It refers to the pattern of prayer used by

Jews before meals. Biblical scholars debate whether the
Last Supper celebrated by Jesus in the Upper Room before his betrayal and crucifixion was an actual Passover
meal. We know it was eaten around the time of the
Passover, a feast that commemorates God's deliverance of
Israel. The Passover covenant was instituted and kept
with the blood of an unblemished lamb. The sacrifice of
lambs as a thank-offering or sin-offering became a characteristic of temple worship and was seen as effecting a
change in the divine-human relationship. It is not surpris-
ing that Jesus, whom John the Baptist called "the Lamb of
God who takes away the sin of the world," came to be referred to as the Paschal (Passover) Lamb. In his instruction to the church at Corinth, Paul wrote, "As often as you
eat this bread and drink the cup you proclaim the Lord's
death until he comes." The meal that Jesus commanded
his followers to eat "in remembrance of me" was a regular and focal point of Christian worship from the very beginning, not only observed concurrent with the Jewish
Passover. Having the Eucharist regularly not only followed the Lord's command; it was understood as being a
meal taken in fellowship with the risen Christ; it allowed
Jesus' followers to participate in the effects of the original
action (such as forgiveness of sin), and it offered a fore-
taste of the messianic banquet in the age to come.

6. The early Christians sang praise to God in their worship
(see Mark 14:26; Acts 16:25; Col. 3:16). The music included
the Psalms, other Old Testament poetry, and composi-
tions about the life, death, and resurrection of Jesus
Christ. The church inherited some of the musical traditions of Jewish worship, in which a leader might sing a
verse and a congregation respond with a repeated refrain.
The oldest distinctively Christian hymns refer to Christ in
the third person; for example, Philippians 2:5–11. This
hymn proclaims the gospel in miniature and exhorts worshipers to praise Jesus Christ. As early as the third century,
however, Hippolytus and others began writing hymns addressed to the second person of the Trinity. This means
that, instead of hymns that talked *about* Jesus ("at the

name of Jesus every knee shall bow . . ."), the new hymns spoke *to* Jesus ("O gracious light . . . . O Jesus Christ, holy and blessed. . . ."). The hymns based on Old Testament texts spoke of God in both second and third person and were written from a variety of life experiences to the sovereign God.

In looking to the Bible for guidance concerning our worship, we should be aware of the variety of influences upon the worship of the first Christians. From the brief overview above, for example, it is evident that the sacrificial element of temple worship, the didactic nature of synagogue services, the zeal of Old Testament prophets, the intimacy of table fellowship, and, above all, the person and work of Jesus Christ shaped the liturgical practice of the early church. It is also helpful to keep in mind that although some of what the Bible says about worship is prescriptive (1 Cor. 11, for example), giving the reader-listener instruction about the "right" way to worship, in other places the Bible is merely describing what was done in a particular time and place (Acts 1:12–14). These texts do not enjoin us to follow the same pattern.

Historical Foundations for Christian Worship

A responsible theology of worship takes into account what the church has done through the ages. It seeks to understand what we have inherited from Christians who lived before us. For example, there has recently been considerable discussion in some Protestant denominations about the names and epithets we use for God. In most congregations, there are men and women who favor the traditional trinitarian formula—"Father, Son, and Holy Spirit"—in prayers and rituals of the church. When reading the Bible aloud, they do not change references to God as "He" to other, non–gender oriented designations. Their reasons for this vary. They may believe changing trinitarian language destroys understanding or muddies the internal relationship of the three persons of the trinity to one another. Because of their high regard for the authority of the Bible, they may distrust tampering with its familiar language. However, most congregations also have men and women who believe the fact God is neither male nor female should be emphasized, particularly in a culture where there has been sex discrimination. They may believe the feminine attributes of and epithets for the divine found in the Bible should be recovered and used.

The question of inclusive language about God is a complex and significant one. It also concerns more than gender. It focuses on our understanding of the nature of the Trinity and the way we worship. Throughout history, the church has dealt with this question in a variety of ways. For instance, Julian of Norwich and other medieval theologians lifted up the maternal aspects of Jesus' nature. Other Christians have focused on holy wisdom as a feminine attribute of God or have used feminine pronouns for the Holy Spirit. This question will no doubt continue to challenge Christians at worship in years to come.

Other worship practices that should direct us to our roots are the age at which people are baptized, whether wine or grape juice is used in Holy Communion, and who may speak or officiate in a worship service. This is not to suggest that we must always do things the way they were done in the past, but we must recognize that the past has shaped who we are and what we do. Some books that may help you understand more about the history of Christian worship practices, and your denomination in particular, are listed at the end of this book (see "For Further Reading"). Your pastor, church librarian, or denominational publishing house may be able to recommend other works to aid in understanding Christian worship.

Denominational Foundations for Christian Worship

The heritage and standards of your particular denomination and the customs of your local congregation are inextricably linked to what the church has done in the past. The troubled church member mentioned earlier knows how it feels when a newcomer does not take into account the cherished traditions of a worshiping community. Although meaning no harm, the new pastor had run roughshod over some persons' feelings. If the minister had discussed with the worship committee the church's heritage and his understanding of worship, much misunderstanding probably could have been avoided.

What is your knowledge of denominational standards and local custom? You can check by asking yourself some of the following questions:

1. For longtime members: Is the order of service the same now as it was when our last pastor was here? If not, what changes have taken place? Does our denomination prescribe a particular order of service?
2. Are people baptized by sprinkling, pouring, or immersion in this church? Are babies baptized? What people (other than the minister and the person being baptized) have special parts in the baptismal ritual? What do they do?
3. How often is the Lord's Supper (or Eucharist) celebrated in this church? Is the frequency decreed by the denomination, the pastor, or local custom? What kinds of bread and wine or juice are used in the sacrament, and why? How do people receive the bread and wine, and who decides how this is done?
4. How does our Sunday morning service differ from that of _____ (a nearby church of the same denomination)? How do we account for the differences?
5. How does our Sunday morning service differ from that of _____ (the nearest church of another denomination)?
6. Other than Christmas and Easter, what are the most important days in the worship life of our congregation? What makes these days important?
7. What recent change(s) in our church's worship have been most popular? Why?
8. What recent change(s) in our church's worship have been least popular? Why?

Decision-making in a Christian Theology of Worship

It is difficult to describe what is "right and true and reasonable" in the theology and practice of worship. Looking to the words of Jesus may help. In Luke 6 and 13, Jesus was criticized by the Pharisees for healing people and plucking grain on the Sabbath. His response indicated that the Pharisees were more interested in fulfilling the letter of the law than in doing what was good and merciful. In Matthew 23, we read of Jesus' criticizing those who made a show of worship, those who tithed but ignored justice and mercy and faith, and those who were hypocrites. In the Sermon on the Mount, Jesus warned listeners not to practice piety for the praise of those around them. From these brief citations, one might conclude that these "right and true" things should be characteristic of Christian worship: It should not be for show. Worship is not something we do for ourselves in order to feel good about ourselves. It should not bully or coerce people. Worship is not a way of gaining favor with God but is done out of love and devotion for God. Christian worship is not a substitute for acting with mercy and justice toward others outside of worship.

It is not hard to imagine how these ideas may be brought to bear on the planning, leadership, and evaluation of worship in a local church. The integrity of worship is not measured by how much money is spent—or how little. The value of the service is not measured by the number of words spoken. Worship does not depend on how much ministerial or lay power is exercised, how entertained members and visitors are, or how satisfied people are with themselves afterwards. It is not good worship if the congregation is confused or intimidated by the leader(s) or if the most they can do is go through the motions because they do not understand or do not agree with what is happening. Something has gone wrong if those who come to worship are prevented or discouraged from participating in what the community of faith is doing.

This is not to say a good theology of worship consists of paying attention to a list of don'ts. The previous catalog of things that can go awry in planning and evaluating worship can actually liberate congregations from mistaken or unworthy agendas. It urges us readers to examine again the words of Jesus in Luke 6 and 13 and consider positive corollaries to what he said: First, *the church's worship will always be aimed at*

pleasing and praising God. As God's creation, established by
Jesus Christ, both worship and worshipers belong to God.
This principle will enable a worship planning committee to
be discerning when someone wants to add to or change
something in the morning service. For example, one church
observed Scout Sunday every year. The scouting groups that
met in the building, along with their leaders, were invited to
attend the service that Sunday, and special recognition was
given to the adult leaders. Was this a "right and reasonable
and true" course of action? It depends on who the leaders
are, the relationship of the congregation to the scouting
groups, and the nature of the recognition. If the scouting
program is understood as one aspect of the church's ministry to children and youth, and the Christian scout leaders
understand their role as one way of expressing their commitment to serve Christ, and if the recognition planned takes
the form of dedication of leaders, renewal of a covenant relationship, or thanks to God for their work, this event may
have a legitimate place in Christian worship. On the other
hand, if the scout groups merely occupy space in the church
building, or if the leaders have no religious commitment, or
the recognition planned is solely to thank and praise the
leaders or advertise scouting as an end in itself, the Scout
Sunday observance has no legitimate place in Christian worship because it does not aim to praise and please God.

Here, then, is a second positive corollary to Jesus' words
that may guide theology and the planning of true and reasonable worship: *The faith expressed and nurtured during worship will seek expression outside worship.* Just as good worship
is people gathered to respond with devotion to what God
has done ("We love, because [God] first loved us"; 1 John
4:19), it tries to bring all of life into conformity and relationship with the Lord. In this way, the worshiping congregation
takes part in God's ongoing redemptive activity, showing by
deeds what is right and true. For instance, a worship committee may ask whether coming activities, often described in
the bulletin, reflect the faith being expressed during the worship service. The incongruity between a sermon on the para-
ble of the lost sheep and a schedule of "fenced-in pasture"

activities is obvious. For example, consider an announcement that "the Men's Prayer Group will meet on Tuesday at its usual time." A visitor cannot participate in this prayer group, because he does not know where, what time, and on what terms it meets. Fenced-in pasture activities may also be those that serve the already-churched but indicate no sense of mission or ministry to those outside the congregation. A worship service that suggests a variety of ways, places, and times to respond to divine nudging *after* the postlude will strengthen both worship and ministry.

This principle is tied closely to the third corollary to Jesus' condemnation of hypocrisy: *A true and right theology of worship will not fabricate or maintain artificial hierarchies among the worshipers but will confess our common identity as sinners in need of grace before the One we worship.* Enabled by the Holy Spirit, this acknowledgment of common identity puts aside other distinctions and enables worshipers to move toward oneness in Christ (see Gal. 3:28) and love one another as Christ has loved us. The Ash Wednesday liturgy used in many traditions bears out this principle. Sin, the universal human predicament, is announced in the recitation of Psalm 51; it is underscored in the imposition of ashes with the pronouncement, "Remember that you are dust, and to dust you shall return," and with the everlasting invitation, "Repent, and believe the Gospel." The smudge of dark ash on each worshiper's forehead is a visible reminder of the common identity and hope all share. A responsible theology or plan for worship acknowledges rather than obscures or denies this truth.

Claiming Symbols and Experience in a Christian Theology of Worship

A responsible theology of worship has meaning in the experience of the individual and congregation. It is not bound to the past but draws sustenance from it. It celebrates the ways God has spoken and acted in the lives of those who participate in it. It recalls, in the best biblical tradition how the mighty acts of God build the community and help it

grow. It recognizes symbolic acts and words that enable people to enter wholeheartedly into worship in the present. For
example, one extended family not given to emotional dis-
play nonetheless customarily closed their infrequent family
get-togethers by singing "God Be With You Till We Meet
Again." This song said for them what they could not articulate individually. When they heard or sang the song in other
contexts, it not only functioned to reinforce kinship ties but
also provided them with a sense of what it is to be part of
the communion of saints. The benefits of this symbol far out-
weighed criticism that the song is oversentimental, repeti-
tive, or outdated.

A second example concerns a congregation that had always had the Eucharist served to them in the pews. They decided it was time to bring variety into the service. Since they
had communion on the first Sunday of every month, they decided they would offer it three different ways on a rotating
basis. One month it would be served as it always had been.
The second month, communicants would come forward and
kneel as they were given morsels of bread and individual
cups. The third month, the Eucharist would be served by
intinction (communicants walking by the servers in single
file and dipping the bread in the wine).

There was negative response to this change, but the worship committee held its ground. As it happened, one Communion Sunday was also set aside as a day to honor the
church's oldest members, many of whom rarely were able to
attend church. This happened to be a Sunday when the worshipers were to kneel to receive communion. People in that
congregation are still talking about that service and how
many people were upset by it. Hurt feelings might well have
been avoided if the changes in the service had been announced and explained in advance, along with the assurance
that provision would be made for those who could not
kneel. As it was, the special guests were confused about the
changes in the service, and some found it difficult to kneel at
the chancel rail. They were left not with delight at the
church's expanded liturgical repertoire but with the feeling
it was not the same church. They felt that the pastor did not

understand their needs, and perhaps they no longer really belonged there.

This is not to suggest a good theology of worship must worship the past or that no changes should be made. Rather, just as our Lord used the stuff of everyday life for his teaching and for the sacraments, so should we. In planning worship we should look for and give thanks for the presence of God expressed in the language and experiences of those who have come to praise their Maker.

Evaluation of Your Theology of Worship

Assessing Our Situation

The following questions deal with your understanding of worship and how worship is conducted in your congregation. Please answer these the best you can by making a check in the appropriate place.

1. Does our denomination have standards for worship which it expects congregations to follow?
   _____yes   _____uncertain   _____no

2. Do members of our congregation tend to have strong feelings about the worship service?
   _____yes   _____uncertain   _____no

3. Do the members tend to express their feelings about the worship service to the appropriate person(s)?
   _____yes   _____uncertain   _____no

4. Do laypersons regularly have a part in the planning and leadership of the worship service?
   _____yes   _____uncertain   _____no

5. Do you think the members of your church find the service of worship meaningful?
   _____yes   _____uncertain   _____no

6. Do you think the members find the service of worship helpful in their daily lives?
   _____yes   _____uncertain   _____no

7. Does the service of worship from time to time affirm our denominational heritage?
   _____yes   _____uncertain   _____no

8. Is communion celebrated on a regular schedule?
   _____yes   _____uncertain   _____no
9. Do the members feel that communion is celebrated about the right number of times per year?
   _____yes   _____uncertain   _____no
10. Is attendance the same or higher on the Sundays when communion is celebrated?
    _____yes   _____uncertain   _____no
11. Are baptisms perceived to be a meaningful part of the service of worship?
    _____yes   _____uncertain   _____no
12. Are the members generally satisfied with the way our pastor leads worship?
    _____yes   _____uncertain   _____no

Now go back over your answers to the questions and give each a score. Write in the scores in the spaces below.

Give each "yes" a score of 3, each "uncertain" a score of 2, and each "no" a score of 1. If you could not answer the question give it a score of 0.

Question	Score
One	_____
Two	_____
Three	_____
Four	_____
Five	_____
Six	_____
Seven	_____
Eight	_____
Nine	_____
Ten	_____
Eleven	_____
Twelve	_____
Total	_____

Add the scores. The total may range from 0 (the weakest score) to 36 (the strongest score). How do the scores given by the members of your group compare with each other?

Discussing the Issues

1. What do you understand should happen in a service of worship?

2. How does this happen in your church?

3. What changes would you like to see made in the worship service in your church?

Responding to the Issues

If most of your group's members gave very high scores for the first section, your church may have addressed the question of its worship ministry recently, with happy results. However, this could also mean that the congregation is ingrown or set in its ways. A good way to determine whether this is the case is to focus your attention on the third question for discussion. If no one has suggestions for change, your church may unconsciously be shutting out or not giving voice to people with new ideas. If scores in the first section were consistently low, it may be that your congregation is fairly new or made up of people from differing backgrounds with different expectations. In any case, you are off to a good start by giving attention to your theologies of worship.

2. The Role of the Laity in Worship

Consider these two scenes depicting the role of the laity in Christian worship.

It is Sunday evening. A Christian woman sits in her kitchen, watching a worship service on the portable black-and-white television on the counter. The preacher is a handsome middle-aged man, well dressed but not flashy. His voice and body language communicate intensity and compassion. The woman has turned the volume down quite low so the preacher's voice will not disturb family members watching another television in the living room. From time to time a Bible verse will flash on the screen, or the camera will focus on the quiet, attentive audience in the television studio. When the preacher finishes, a small choir stands and beautifully executes a contemporary arrangement of a familiar hymn. The woman watching the television jots down the telephone number given out at the end of the anthem, then she reaches for the phone and calls to make a pledge. Her contribution will help keep the program she enjoys on the air.

It is Sunday morning. A small congregation expects the guest preacher any moment. Their own pastor is out of town. The custodian comes early to turn up the heat in the sanctuary. A member arrives with the flowers she has arranged for the altar table. The lay leader checks with various people in the congregation to make sure the announcements for the service are in order. Two elderly members stand at the door, handing hymnbooks to each person who enters. There are no bulletins. The youth fellowship adviser keeps an eye open for any teenagers who wander in so they may sit together as a group. When the guest preacher arrives, she is greeted by two laypersons who take her to the vestry. They have already made sure there is a glass of water in the pulpit, and now they ask the guest preacher for the hymn numbers and lessons. They go over the details of the service with her and give her a copy of a list of the persons for whom prayer is requested that week. One of the men leads in prayer for the preacher and those who have come to worship. During the service, lay people read the lessons, lead the singing, make the announcements, take up the offering, and assist any visitors who need help following the order of service.

Both these scenes are real. In the former, the worshiper is isolated and passive. Lay participation is limited to making a phone call, writing a check, and perhaps praying for the minister and the station that broadcasts the service. The viewer may have a sense of knowing the preacher, but it is not reciprocal. The worshipers do not greet one another, pray, work together, or know anything about one another. In the latter scene, worship is corporate and participatory. The people at worship communicate with each other and with the preacher before, after, and perhaps during the service. Lay participation is limited only by the denomination's restrictions concerning preaching and celebrating the Eucharist.

Unfortunately, in recent years there have been two trends in worship that are illustrated more by the woman watching television than the congregation involved in every aspect of the service. The first trend is to focus undue attention on the person at the pulpit or microphone while minimizing the importance and contribution of other people to the total worship service. Lay people serve as ushers and may perform choral music, but most in the congregation do not believe they have any say about what happens in worship. They do not have a deep investment in the worshiping community. This fosters the second trend, which is a consumer attitude toward Sunday morning. The worshiper views the service as a program or performance. Instead of engaging in an activity with others to the glory of God, the audience decides whether or not to tune in again. In this situation, the minister's self-image may shift, often unconsciously, to that of soloist.

Taking an active role in worship means more than a preacher's or minister's summoning the courage to speak before a crowd on Sunday morning. In this chapter, ways are suggested for lay people to understand better what happens in the worship service, to evaluate what is currently taking place in their churches, and to plan with the ordained clergy for a vital worship ministry.

Understanding What Is Happening in Worship

A frequently overlooked resource for understanding what is happening in your worship today is the church's oral tradition. Important information can be secured by talking to longtime members, reading old bulletins stored in the church office, reviewing former pastors' records of ministerial service, and examining decisions made by the memorial and building committees. This will help people understand what they have inherited, what needs to be changed, what can be done, and what everyone will have to put up with until further notice.

For example, ushers at one church struggled every Sunday morning with young adults who insisted on sitting in the balcony even though half the pews on the main floor were empty. The ushers knew the sanctuary would look fuller if they could get this stubborn group to join the rest of the congregation. The head usher even introduced a resolution at a board meeting to close the balcony, saying it would not only enhance worship but be one less place for the custodian to clean. Then someone who had been at the church for a generation realized why the group would not abandon the balcony: This was where key members of the group sat when they were in church membership class. Just as it was the point of entry for them as teenagers, it had become the point of entry for persons currently newcomers in that age group. The ushers and others at the meeting subsequently redirected their efforts from trying to move these worshipers downstairs to trying to make them feel more a part of worship and fellowship activities.

In another church, the program planning committee was asked to report on comments about worship in order to set goals for the future. A fairly new member of the committee said he thought the sanctuary was unattractive; the chancel furniture was blond wood in a fairly plain style, while the woodwork around the windows and the pews had a much darker finish and appeared to be older. He wondered if money or a work crew could be raised to make all the woodwork in the worship space match. Longtime church members smiled. One of them replied, "Money isn't the issue. We voted several years ago to have all the furniture refinished, but by the time we finished the chancel area, so many people objected to it that we decided not to continue the project." When the newcomer asked if the chancel furnishings could then be stained dark again, he was told, "We could, but you see, the congregation was split on this issue. Half of them liked it light, and the other half liked it dark. Leaving it as it is has been a compromise. I suppose we could put the issue to the congregation again."

In the first of these examples, turning to the history contained in the congregation's oral tradition resulted in learning to live with a situation. In the second, discovering the reasons for the present situation led to reopening the issue for discussion. A second avenue for greater understanding of worship among the laity in your church is inviting the pastor or a denominational representative to speak to a particular issue pertaining to worship. For example, when a new hymnbook is published, most denominations furnish audiovisual resources and sometimes trained speakers to introduce the worship materials.

A new pastor inevitably does things just a bit differently from the previous one. Much misunderstanding and resentment can be avoided if changes in the format or content of worship are described *before* the worship takes place. This may be done through a lay-edited church newsletter, an announcement before the service, or by discussion of the new material in church school.

Church school can aid people at all age levels in understanding worship by periodically offering for study some aspect of the Sunday service. An effort can be made to select church school materials with lessons that are coordinated with the texts used in worship each week. Children's classes may include brief worship services so that students learn by doing. Classes and fellowship groups may decide to visit services in other traditions from time to time to understand what is distinctive about their own church's way of doing things. They may also study what is unique about worship in their church as distinguished from others of the same tradition. It may be, for example, that your worship is really built around the church's music program because the congregation is blessed with a gifted music leader, a substantial music budget, or lay people who are particularly interested in participating in this ministry. The schedule of services and their relationship to the church's Christian education program may reflect the special needs and desires of the church's constituency, or it may be a cumbersome carryover from an earlier period. Some large churches, for instance, schedule ninety minutes for the adult meeting, with a forty-five to sixty minute combination Bible lesson–homily while children and youth are in church school classes. Whenever you come across an emphasis or practice in worship that sets a congregation apart from other traditions and other churches of its own denomination, you will do well to investigate the reasons behind it. This prepares an individual or committee to make evaluative statements about that aspect of worship.

Evaluating What Is Happening in Worship

Evaluation tends to create anxiety in those being evaluated. However, there are a number of nonthreatening, nonadversarial ways a church school class, worship committee, or other group within the church can evaluate their present patterns of worship. A nonadversarial method is important because the goal of an evaluation is not to get rid of the pastor or see who can wield the most power; it is rather to explore and strengthen a corporate activity. It is not conducive to worship if the pastor and one or more groups in the congregation are busy defending turf.

A constructive, objective way to begin an evaluation of present worship practices is to keep track of what resources and acts are currently part of the Sunday service. Many pastors have a copy of the hymnbook in the church office in which the date a particular hymn is used in worship is noted. Choir directors often keep records of what anthems are used each week. If these tallies are made available to the group evaluating worship, the group will be able to note trends. They may discover that some selections seem to be used very frequently. Sunday bulletins may be used to study the structure of worship, the type and range of liturgical materials used, and the nature of lay participation. The same few laypersons may have speaking roles in the service and certain themes or worship materials may be overworked. The tallies will also help address complaints and requests regarding worship; for example, if a group in the church is complaining that not enough of the "good old hymns" are being sung, they can be asked to compile a list of their favorites and check it against the annotated hymnbook. The list of requested hymns also becomes a specific suggestion that can be passed on to the pastor or other person who selects music each week.

An alternative way to begin evaluation of current worship and the role of laity is for a group to ask themselves the following: What do we believe is the role of the ordained clergy in worship, and what is/are the role(s) of the laity? To what extent do we expect the pastor to "serve us" a Sunday morning worship service? How do our expectations square with our theology of worship? Quite often such questions reveal a discrepancy between belief about the equality of all persons before God in the church and a belief in the pastor as high priest or mediator, a role which he or she is expected to play on Sunday morning. Further discussion may reveal that laypersons are willing to exercise leadership in other kinds of church work but that they shy away from responsibilities pertaining to worship.

A popular way to evaluate worship is to conduct a congregational survey. Airing opinions is a cathartic experience. Care should be taken to phrase survey questions in a way that doesn't incite animosity and distrust. Worship surveys sometimes mask important issues that should be dealt with in another context. Contrast these two sets of open-ended questions:

Helpful Questions
— What topics or texts would you like to hear addressed in sermons during the next year?
— What part of the service are you most likely to remember later in the week?

"Loaded" or Unhelpful Questions
— What do you think is wrong with our present order of service?
— Is the pastor fulfilling his or her responsibility to minister to us in worship?
— Do you think laywomen should be allowed to read the scriptures during the Sunday morning service?

Ideally, a congregational survey functions not only as a diagnostic tool but also as a method of helping the members develop a sense of ownership of the worship service. In addition, it should provide a foundation for planning and a stimulus to further involvement on the part of laity. For this to happen, there must be consensus among laity and clergy that the questions are helpful and goal oriented.

A final resource for evaluating your worship program is other churches of your tradition. Laity should be encouraged to bring bulletins from other churches they visit and to tell what aspects of the service they would like to see tried at their home church. They should also be invited to talk about what made a negative impression and why. Since laity have far more opportunity to visit other churches than clergy do, they can provide insights and materials to which the pastor and other worship planners might not otherwise have access.

The Role of Laity in Planning Worship

While laity may enjoy the chance to request that a favorite hymn be sung on Sunday morning, very few want to usurp what they believe is the pastor's role in making decisions about worship services: preparing and preaching a sermon, celebrating the sacraments, saying the pastoral prayer or prayer of intercession and thanksgiving, and making week-by-week decisions about the service. Although preaching and leading worship are recognized as being among the primary responsibilities of the pastor, continual deference to the pastor's opinions and ideas can be counterproductive. Not all ordained ministers are educated in preaching and worship. Even those who have graduated from seminary may not have taken courses in these subjects. And even those who took every preaching and worship course offered by the school are not automatically endowed with creativity or omniscience about the gifts and ideas in your congregation. The pastor needs you, the laity, to assist in planning worship that is the best it can be.

What happens Sunday morning is related to everything else that happens in the life of the church. These events include meetings of service groups, or Scouts; church school; prayer circles; outreach ministries; newsletter publication; ecumenical activities, and the like. All these are mainly lay work, and most are lay led. Whether the church officers or the entire congregation plans programs for the future, the life of the congregation will be stronger if those planning worship set joint goals with laity—goals that go beyond increasing attendance and raising the budget. For example, there may be consensus that one goal of the congregation is to attract more young adults to its worship. Hiring a younger minister or asking the choir director to use more contemporary Christian music may not serve the goal. More effective strategies, which depend on lay involvement, may include considering an alternate service to fit the schedule and tastes of this group (without neglecting those of the people already part of the congregation), offering nursery care for the children of young adults during the worship service, or arranging for peer visitation of the young adults who have already attended a service. While we do not think of house visitation and baby-sitting as acts of worship as such, they are lay activities that strengthen the Sunday morning service.

Another step in evaluating the role of laity in worship is for the group using this book to list each person who plays a part in making your Sunday service come together. The list should include everyone from the person who plugs in the public address system to the altar guild member who washes the communion cups after the service. List the tasks pertaining to worship each layperson is performing. This may reveal how more people could be involved and thus have a greater stake in what happens on Sunday morning. For example, if one pillar of the church is responsible for so many different jobs that without his or her presence the worship service would collapse, it is time to reexamine the structure and consider how the weight of responsibility can be shared by many.

When the pastor and members decide that the laity should have a more active role in the planning and leading of worship, the temptation is to think of such involvement in limited, predictable ways, such as having lay members serve as acolytes, greeters, and ushers; read the lessons; or provide special music. This kind of lay involvement is good, but it should be the beginning rather than the end of your plans for greater participation. Here is a sample of ideas for employing the creativity and talents of your members in worship:

— A Bible study group that uses the lectionary texts for each week may contribute to the next Sunday's sermon by supplying the pastor with insights from the group's discussion.
— A church school class studying the prayers used in worship can compose invocations and collects for use in the Sunday service.
— A musician in the congregation whose schedule precludes choir practice can nonetheless perhaps arrange or compose music for use in worship, and instrumentalists may perform it or teach it to the congregation.
— Instead of buying banners from a church supply store,

textile artists in the congregation can design and make vestments, banners, paraments, and other visual aids for worship.

— A children's group or class in the church can take responsibility for making the bread for the Eucharist.

— A church school class might present a liturgical drama based on the day's texts or a seasonal theme.

— Any interested worshiper may be able to compose a two- or three-sentence meditation for the congregation to read during the prelude.

All these activities, of course, would be screened by the worship planning committee, evaluated for their congruence with the church's theology of worship, and coordinated by the pastor so as to avoid making the Sunday service look like a disjointed talent show.

People feel far greater investment in things they do than in things they merely see or hear. Therefore it is in the church's best interest to provide as many opportunities as possible for lay participation in worship. This does not blur the distinction between clergy and laity but makes their roles in worship complementary.

Evaluation of the Role of Laity in Worship

Assessing Our Situation

The following questions deal with your understanding of the role of the laity in your congregation. Please answer these the best you can by making a check in the appropriate place.

1. Does a worship committee or equivalent group discuss long-term goals concerning worship?
   _____yes   _____uncertain   _____no

2. Is there coordination between the planning of worship and the planning of other church activities and goals?
   _____yes   _____uncertain   _____no

3. Have lay people participated in leadership or worship in new ways within the last three years?
   _____yes   _____uncertain   _____no

4. Does a representative cross-section of our congregation have opportunity to contribute to the Sunday morning service?

_____yes   _____uncertain   _____no

5. Are there regular opportunities, other than the Sunday morning service, for laity to plan and lead worship (for instance, men's, women's and youth meetings; church school classes, mid-week services, and so forth)?

_____yes   _____uncertain   _____no

6. If our church has ushers, do they continue ushering throughout the service?

_____yes   _____uncertain   _____no

7. Are hymns ever accompanied by some instrument besides our regular organ or piano?

_____yes   _____uncertain   _____no

8. Do lay people ever lead prayers in our church, either before or during the worship service?

_____yes   _____uncertain   _____no

9. If the ordained minister became ill during the first ten minutes of Sunday morning worship, could the service go on without him or her?

_____yes   _____uncertain   _____no

10. Are the pastor and congregation generally satisfied with the current level of lay involvement in worship?

_____yes   _____uncertain   _____no

Now go back over your answers to the questions and give each a score. Write in the scores in the spaces below. Give each "yes" a score of 3, each "uncertain" a score of 2, and each "no" a score of 1. If you could not answer the question, give it a score of 0.

Question	Score
One	_____
Two	_____
Three	_____
Four	_____
Five	_____
Six	_____
Seven	_____

Eight   _____
Nine   _____
Ten   _____

Total   _____

Add the scores. The total may range from 0 (the weakest score) to 30 (the strongest score). How do the scores given by the members of your group compare with each other?

Discussing the Issues

1. What printed information about worship is available to laity in the newsletter, church library, tract rack, or church school material?

2. What opportunities for feedback about worship does the pastor have at present?

3. What people in your church could be utilized to enhance your worship?

4. Has passive viewing of religious television programs had any impact on lay participation in your church's worship?

Responding to the Issues

As you compare scores and discuss the questions above, it is possible conversation will center on what the pastor and one or two laypersons are doing, particularly if there is some dissatisfaction about what your answers revealed. And there may indeed be a problem person in your congregation. Rather than allowing one person to become a scapegoat, however, try to look at the bigger picture. If there is frustration with the nature and degree of lay participation, identify how this situation came about. For example, if people are disgruntled that Jerry has been asked to speak on Laity Sunday for the ninth year running, do not jump to the conclusion that Jerry is a powermonger and ought to be taken down a peg. Ask how the pattern began. It may be that Jerry wishes someone else would do the job but cannot say no when approached by an unimaginative committee. Keep in mind that unrest concerning lay participation in worship may point to other important issues in the life of the congregation that really do not have much to do with worship as such. If the pastor is not part of the group working through this book, make the fruits of your discussion, and perhaps the scores, available to him or her and encourage continued dialogue about these issues.

3. The Worship Setting

Christians nearly always gather to worship in sacred space. People can have memorable religious experiences anywhere (at tent meetings, while singing around a campfire, and even in less likely settings), but most religions and certainly Christianity have more permanent sites for regular worship. Even in missionary situations, such as that of the Celtic church prior to St. Augustine of Canterbury, crosses were erected at outdoor preaching places (often former sites of pagan rituals), which became sacred space for Christian worship.[1] Today the overwhelming majority of congregations have a building that they own or on which they are making mortgage payments.

This chapter will first examine the relationship between the worship setting and the congregation's theology of worship. Next, questions will be posed about your church's worship setting and what it communicates explicitly and implicitly. This will lead into considerations congregations should take into account when they are planning to build worship space or change the one they already have.

Theology of Worship and Sacred Space

Most Christians in the United States have had the experience of attending a wedding at an unfamiliar church or of driving by a church and saying to themselves, "Who built that?" Perhaps the design of the church reminded you of a beached whale, a bank, or the Taj Mahal. On the other hand, it may have evoked a sense of satisfaction or the recognition that *this* is the way a church is supposed to look.

Chances are that the worship space that impresses you as bizarre, unsuitable, or unattractive reflects an understanding of worship that is different from your own. Different aspects of worship have been regarded as particularly important in various times and places in the church's history. Dominant theological concerns have found expression in the part of a building set aside as sacred space.

During the first few centuries of the church's history, Christians did not have the freedom to construct or designate settings exclusively for worship. They gathered to worship in such places as private homes, catacombs, or even prisons. The oldest preserved Christian worship space is a third-century house-church in Dura-Europos on the Euphrates River. Interesting features of this square place of worship are a small platform at one end of the room where the altar table and perhaps presider's chair were located, a large baptistery covered with a canopy, and frescoes on the walls.[2] No traces remain of a pulpit. From the physical setting, we may make the following observations about the theology of worship of the congregation:

1. The sacrament of baptism played an important role, since the large font and canopy were permanent fixtures.
2. The Eucharist played an important role, because the place for the table was visible to all in the worship space.
3. The religious frescoes suggest that the arts were not only regarded as a way to glorify God in worship but also as a means of teaching the congregation the faith.
4. Preaching may not have been understood or done in the same way as it is today, given the lack of evidence for it.

Dura-Europos is an early and simple worship space. It is fairly easy to read for theological clues. The fact that it existed before Christianity became legal testifies to the importance of sacred space for the worshiping community. The development over time of increasingly sophisticated worship space bears witness to a changing relationship between church and state. This illustrated the diversity of theological concerns and beliefs as to what was important when the congregation gathered for worship and concerning the controversy over the roles of laity and ordained clergy.

After Constantine declared Christianity lawful and respectable, Western churches began to take on a shape indicative of their new relationship to the government. Sacred space took the shape of the basilica, or Roman law court: a rectangular building with a semicircular, elevated apse at one end.[3] The table, pulpit, and leaders of worship were located in the apse. There were no seats for the congregation in the nave (the long part of the rectangle). This model for worship space suggests a clearer division between the roles of laity and ordained clergy in worship than was evident in Dura-Europos. It is the forerunner of a generally longitudinal development of worship space in the Western church that was not seriously challenged until the Reformation. Consider a soaring Gothic church constructed in the Middle Ages with its long center aisle, elevated chancel, pulpit, altar table, screen separating the choir from the congregation, arches pointing toward heaven, and glowing stained-glass windows. Some theological assumptions inherent in this design are:

1. God is transcendent, holy, and majestic.
2. There is a church within the church (that is, choir and clergy set apart from the congregation).
3. Being present when the priest celebrates the Eucharist is more important than seeing what is happening or hearing the words that are said.
4. Visual aids inspire and instruct the worshiper, who is often illiterate or does not own a Bible or prayerbook.
5. Receiving the Eucharist is less important than the fact that the priest celebrates it.

Another example of the relationship between theology of worship and its setting may be helpful in learning how to understand what is being communicated to those who see your church for the first time. The Akron style sanctuary was considered the latest in church design in the early part of the twentieth century. Somewhat reminiscent of the New

England Congregational meeting house, the Akron style is characterized by a rectangular room with a prominent central pulpit in one corner, visible organ pipes behind the pulpit, curved pews, large doors at the rear or side that can be opened for overflow crowds and/or Sunday school space, a small and easily moved altar table below the pulpit, and possibly a gallery to allow a large crowd to hear the preacher.

This design is not known for utilizing visual art. Other than perhaps the Lord's Prayer, Ten Commandments, or Bible verses painted where all can see them, there are minimal visual aids to educate or edify the worshiper. In this respect the style is quite different from the Gothic cathedral or early Christian house-church. The Akron style is not in favor today, partly because churches would rather schedule additional services on Sunday morning as needed than erect a large and expensive auditorium.

Some of the theological assumptions being communicated by this setting for worship include:

1. Proclamation of the Word is the most important part of worship, as indicated by the centrality and size of the pulpit. The preacher is the key figure in the worship service.
2. Hearing is the most important sense in worship, as indicated by the concern for acoustics and the visible organ pipes.
3. The sacraments do not play an important role in worship, as evidenced by the diminutive altar table and absence of a fixed baptismal font or pool.
4. The congregation worships by sitting still and listening to what is said or by standing and singing. Fixed pews and lack of open space suggest this.
5. The preacher, rather than an elaborate church decor, is what you ought to see when you worship God.

Someone who grew up worshiping in an Akron-style setting, a basilica, or a house-church may protest, "That isn't my theology of worship at all!" Even so, that is the theology of worship communicated by the layout of the worship space plus the relative sizes and prominence of table, baptistery, pulpit, choir space, and congregational space. Worshipers may adapt themselves to a setting that is not altogether congruent with their theology of worship, of course. The congregation may inherit a sanctuary that reflects the self-understanding and purpose of the members of a previous generation. They may have a strong attachment to a building not for its physical features but because important events in their lives such as baptisms, weddings, and funerals, have occurred there. Even so, it should be kept in mind the building itself makes a theological statement that may invite or repel visitors.

What Does Your Worship Space Communicate?

Every worship setting communicates in plain and subtle ways what the congregation believes about itself, its worship, and its mission. Persons who are about to build, remodel, redecorate, or add memorials to a sanctuary will do well to focus on the more *explicit* theological statements that can be made in a building. If you joined the church recently or inherited worship space designed and built at an earlier time, you may have to consider the implicit theology of worship suggested by design.

First, consider the immediate and fairly obvious conclusions visitors may make when they walk into your place of worship. These hearken back to some of the previous observations made about historic church designs. The *size* of your setting for worship in relation to the rest of the building reflects your congregation's understanding of mission. A one-room country church is suitable for the thirty to fifty persons who attend. It also suggests that worship is the only purpose for which the people gather. An enormous church complex serving several thousand, in which the gymnasium or theater is the single largest room, suggests another theology of worship. The *shape* of the room and division of congregational space, choir space, and other features will suggest the kinds of worship that occur in the church. These elements plus the location of liturgical centers communicate the denomination's and the members' sense of what is most important in the worship service. A cruciform sanctuary with side altars or chapels gives a very different message from a Quaker meetinghouse with no apparent liturgical centers.

A design for worship space that has enjoyed increasing popularity in recent years, particularly since the reforms of Vatican II, is the square or octagonal sanctuary with seating more or less in the round, facing a chancel area that is only slightly elevated for better visibility. Congregational seating may be fixed pews or movable seats, but the distance from the back pew to the chancel is less than in the Akron plan or the Gothic church. The aisles are wider than in earlier designs and give a general feeling of spaciousness. There may or may not be kneelers, but there will be racks in the pews for worship materials. In the chancel area the pulpit, font, and altar table are balanced in terms of size and prominence, and the altar table is free-standing. Liturgical symbols are fewer and simpler but are apt to be motifs repeated in the building's shape, decoration on paraments, design of chancel furniture, and the like.

The shape of such a room for worship makes several theological statements:

1. Intimacy and community with others attending the service are important. It is not enough to see and hear those leading worship; seeing others in the congregation is also an essential part of worship.
2. Worship has more than one focus, evidenced by the equal prominence given to pulpit, altar table, and font.
3. Worship leaders arise from the Christian community (it is impossible to get to the chancel without passing through the pews).

Finally, the functional and decorative furnishings say a great deal about your church's theology of worship. If yours is a Protestant church with a sanctuary light, kneelers, and prayer books as well as hymnals in the pew rack, you are probably Episcopalian. If your worship space is rectangular, with the pulpit above the altar table in a fenced-in area on one of the long sides of the rectangle, the pews are on three sides of the chancel area, and the decor is simple, it is likely you are in an eighteenth-century Congregational meeting-house. To the modern worshiper not familiar with it, this setting may communicate a variety of things; positive associations may include simplicity, commonsense ideas of the people who built the church, or the traditional American values associated with Norman Rockwell paintings. Its lack of ornamentation, its fixed pews and fenced-off liturgical centers may also communicate austerity, seriousness, or rigidity on the part of those who worship there.

If there is a pastoral scene, possibly with a river, painted on a wall above a liturgical center, chances are yours is a church that practices baptism by immersion. People will *expect* a different style of worship from that which occurs in the Congregational meetinghouse, and if it does not happen, they may be confused or try to account for the discrepancy by guessing that the building was inherited from another tradition, that things have changed a lot since they grew up, or some other factor. The flexibility of congregational seating, number of seats for worship leaders, attention to lighting, sophistication of the sound system, and amount and type of liturgical art all suggest your theology of worship.

The Willow Creek Community Church in suburban Chicago, one of the largest and fastest-growing congregations in the United States, has a worship space that is difficult to distinguish from a concert hall. The approximately five thousand theater seats are bolted to a sloping floor. There are no hymnals or racks for books. Instead of a chancel in front, there is a large stage with state-of-the-art sound equipment. A clear Plexiglas pulpit is placed on the stage when it is time for the sermon. The walls are bare of decoration, but huge windows on either side of the stage offer a view of rolling countryside and a small lake. (However, the manicured lawns suggest a golf course rather than untouched wilderness.) A dozen wide-screen television monitors allow those in the gallery to see the preacher's face. Willow Creek Church has two constituencies (and corresponding worship services). The first includes church shoppers and searchers who are not committed Christians. Their worship service is more performance oriented than participatory. Preaching, which is informal, colloquial, and upbeat, often focuses on the needs, problems, and feelings of those who attend. The second consists of those who are active, committed members of the congregation. In this worship service, more of the music is congregational singing and less is performance. The Bible is used explicitly in the sermon, and worshipers are addressed as those who are already part of the church. There are challenges to faithful living and involvement in the church's many outreach ministries. What theology of worship and understanding of God are suggested by this setting for worship? Does the setting fit one group better than another? If so, why?

Think about the more subtle statements your congregation makes about worship with its sanctuary. The greater the *distance* between the pulpit and the normally occupied congregational seating, the greater the sense of isolation of the preacher from the parishioners. Eye contact is possible only up to fifty-five feet. If your congregation makes a point of sitting beyond that range, the implication is that a sense of intimacy with the ones leading worship is not valued. The amount of care given to the worship setting communicates at a nonverbal level to visitors. A shabby but clean sanctuary presents a more positive view of worship than one in which old bulletins and Sunday school material are left on a rear pew, because the former says worshipers care about the place in which they gather in Jesus' name. Fresh flowers, whether from a member's garden or from a florist, indicate a higher regard for worship than does a plastic bouquet; an implicit difference is communicated about what is real and what is artificial as well as offering back to God a portion of what God has created. There is also the possibility of ongoing ministry after worship if these flowers are taken to someone unable to attend church. Consistency in nonverbal communication about worship diminishes the anxiety a first-time visitor may feel. The presence of a sanctuary lamp, a baptismal tank, ordo calendars and *Gospel Light* tracts in a single building hint at a lack of liturgical identity. Locating the pulpit directly under a basketball hoop or having a painting of Jesus in the Garden of Gethsemane next to the flower sign-up chart may mean worship takes place in a multipurpose room. (For the visitor, such a setting suggests a lack of focus and unintentional—one hopes—humor.) Placing a heavy, dirty chain or other incongruous objects on the altar table may have prophetic symbolism for the members of your congregation, but someone seeing such an object the first time may perceive it as irreverent and shocking and not as the theological statement the congregation intended.

Features to Keep in Mind When Planning or Revising the Worship Setting

Use this section as you walk through the space your congregation uses for worship. Some of the issues raised may seem more mundane than theological, but even the most pragmatic considerations have an impact on your congregation's theology of worship. Your answers will give you an idea of the extent to which a newcomer in the community can participate easily in the Sunday morning service. They will suggest changes that will give a clearer expression to your theology of worship.

A first thing to be considered is how a passerby knows when worship services are held. Many Protestant churches simply have a permanent sign in front of the building giving the name of the church and the denomination. These give the "brand name" but do not provide the potential worshiper with information as to when anything might take place. The impression given is that one needs to be an insider to participate. Listing the times church school and worship services take place will solve this problem.

Churches frequently overlook the opportunity of telling people what is happening by advertising in the yellow pages or local newspaper. If nursery care is available during worship, this information should also be stated in the ad. Your congregation may regard such advertising as an extravagance because there are not enough visitors to justify the expense—but perhaps there would be more visitors if they knew what was happening Sunday morning.

A second consideration is where visitors may park and how they are informed of the way to the sanctuary. Visitors who wish to be inconspicuous will appreciate signs showing them the way to where worship takes place.

The capacity of the sanctuary may reflect the size of the current congregation or expectations for membership growth. Sometimes the projections have been too low, and the building is soon too small. This difficulty may be addressed by having multiple services until long-term plans can be made and implemented. In other cases the expectations for growth are too high, and a building is constructed that remains too large. One congregation of four hundred members assumed it would grow to twelve hundred and built accordingly. The membership leveled off at eight hundred, so the facilities were never fully utilized. Not only is this poor stewardship, it causes low morale among members. A flexible design for worship space might have allowed the congregation to use only part of the room originally designed for worship. The remainder of the space could have been used for coffee hour after the service, for choir rehearsals and a variety of other activities. Large empty spaces in the main worship service convey a negative impression to visitors, who are not likely to remain on board what appears to be a sinking ship.

It is rare that a church building will meet all the needs of a congregation at any given time. Churches and the communities that they serve constantly change. This is a fact of life. Congregations can cope with it by designing worship space with the maximum degree of flexibility and by dealing with available space imaginatively.

The arrangement of liturgical centers and congregational space will dictate, to a large extent, what takes place in worship. The layout of the sanctuary should not fight with the order of service. When it does, the building will always win. For example, asking the whole congregation to sing a hymn and march to their seats for a particular occasion simply will not work if the pews are close together and bolted to the floor, the aisles are relatively narrow, and the traffic pattern is not clear.

Pastoral and congregational care may or may not be evident as you examine the place where you worship. Air con-
ditioning or adequate ventilation, the accessibility of the
sanctuary to handicapped persons, provision for those who
are hearing impaired (hearing aid outlets, a good public address system, someone who can sign the service, or the
availability of tapes after the service) say that all are wel-
come to come and worship God here. Commonplace ameni-
ties such as coat racks, conveniently located drinking
fountains and washrooms, a nearby nursery or crying room,
and a vestibule or other space for fellowship are all visible
indications that the congregation looks for ways to embody
God's love to others. These cost far less than a new church
building, but they help make your worship space one that
"works" for both members and visitors.

Evaluation of the Worship Setting

Assessing Our Situation

The following questions deal with various aspects of the
worship setting and the church building.

1. Does the worship setting suggest that this is sacred
   space?
   _____yes   _____uncertain   _____no
2. Are the liturgical centers (pulpit, altar table, baptistery,
   etc.) visible to everyone who comes to worship?
   _____yes   _____uncertain   _____no
3. Does the liturgical art used enhance the understanding
   of the worshiper and aid in corporate worship?
   _____yes   _____uncertain   _____no
4. Is the size of the worship space appropriate to the congregation and activities taking place there?
   _____yes   _____uncertain   _____no
5. Are the visual clues about worship congruent with the
   congregation's theology of worship?
   _____yes   _____uncertain   _____no
6. Is the worship space well maintained?
   _____yes   _____uncertain   _____no

7. Are the acoustics in the sanctuary adequate?
   _____yes   _____uncertain   _____no

8. Is there provision for persons with special needs, such as the hearing impaired, those in wheelchairs, and so on?
   _____yes   _____uncertain   _____no

9. Is there space that provides opportunity for interaction among worshipers before and after the service?
   _____yes   _____uncertain   _____no

10. Do parking spaces, directional signs, and other features make it easy for visitors to attend worship services?
    _____yes   _____uncertain   _____no

Now go back over your answers to the questions and give each a score. Write in the scores in the spaces below. Give each "yes" a score of 3, each "uncertain" a score of 2, and each "no" a score of 1. If you could not answer the question, give it a score of 0.

Question	*Score*
One	_____
Two	_____
Three	_____
Four	_____
Five	_____
Six	_____
Seven	_____
Eight	_____
Nine	_____
Ten	_____
Total	_____

Add the scores. The total will range from 0 (the weakest score) to 30 (the strongest score). How do the scores given by the members of your group compare with each other?

Discussing the Issues

1. What does the layout of your worship space suggest is the most important part of the service?

2. What part of your sanctuary best expresses the congregation's theology of worship, and what part is least congruent with it?

3. What changes could you make in your current setting for worship that would make it more accessible and attractive to newcomers?

Responding to the Issues

Some of the issues raised in the questions will be relatively easy to address, such as maintaining the worship space or putting up directional signs for visitors. Other issues, such as the degree of congruity between architecture and layout and your theology of worship, may elicit frustration from group members. You may have inherited someone else's dream: worship space that does not fit the congregation's self-understanding, goals in ministry, or budget. If this is the case, you may find it helpful to add a fourth discussion question: For what age or interest group does our worship space pose the greatest difficulty? If you can identify this constituency, ways to work around the liabilities of space may suggest themselves. For example, one small congregation whose young families were frustrated because there was no crying room or crib nursery found a temporary solution by removing a pew near the back of the worship space. This created more space for baby carriages and a low table where small children could color pictures during the service.

4. The Music Used in Worship

The Sunday morning service was over and the people were leaving. As one couple walked home, the wife said, "Wasn't the music great today? The anthem was inspiring; it's good to attend a church where the music is high quality."

A short distance away, two other persons were heading toward their car. One commented with some degree of feeling, "I don't understand why we can't ever sing anything we know. The pastor always seems to select hymns nobody ever heard before. That anthem didn't do anything for me, either."

Church members have strong feelings about the hymns and other music used in worship. In fact, their feelings about the music tend to be stronger than about any other aspect of the worship service. As one disgruntled church member put it, "We know what we like, and we like what we know!" The music committee or choir is often jokingly, but not necessarily incorrectly, referred to as the War Department.

Why is this? One reason is that while most lay people have no desire to preach sermons and no opportunity to lead other acts of worship, they can and do sing favorite religious music in church and other contexts (church camps and retreats, school or family reunions, singing alone or accompanying themselves on piano or guitar, and listening to the radio). During the Advent-Christmas season, they hear familiar religious music even at shopping malls.

A second reason for intense feelings about the music used in worship is that music evokes strong associations with significant events in an individual's life. Hearing a particular hymn or song is a way of remembering or reenacting important events. Wagner's *Lohengrin* may remind Christians more of weddings than operas. "In the Sweet By and By" may evoke bittersweet memories of a loved one's funeral.

A third reason for the strong feelings Christians have about church music is the importance it plays in both worship and faith development. It is not an exaggeration to say that many Christians learn their theology from the hymns they sing. Hymns shape, ratify, and proclaim a worshiper's experience of God. For example, "How Great Thou Art," an immensely popular song in evangelical Protestant traditions, not only expresses the singer's experience of God but also instructs the hearer about ways in which God's presence may be apprehended. It suggests the appropriate response to an encounter with the divine, and it announces the second coming of Christ. The words are not difficult to memorize, and the irregular tune and meter invite the singer's individual interpretations. While many persons love this hymn, others strongly dislike it. It would be difficult to find a single item in liturgy that would do all that one beloved hymn or song does—or that has the potential for causing such division. When the United Methodist Church conducted a survey prior to publishing a new hymnal, "How Great Thou Art" was the hymn that received the most votes for inclusion *and* for exclusion. Loyalty to favorite religious music is intense.

Fourth, singing is one part of worship in which all present can participate by blending their voices toward the common goal of praising God. It is one of the most corporate acts in the church service. Worshipers feel united to one another as well as interacting with God when they sing. The appeal of such activity cannot be overlooked.[1]

It is unfortunate that both clergy and laity often have been very selective in the type of music used. People tend to permit the choir director or the organist to make random decisions as to which instrumental music shall be used as long as their favorite vocal music is sung. Sometimes the importance of organ, piano, or guitar music in the service has been downplayed. The people are then prevented from attaining a deeper understanding and a richer experience of worship. For instance, in one church bulletin the prelude and postlude were usually listed as "Selected." It became a standing joke that "selected" must be the most prolific composer whoever lived because his music was played almost every Sunday! In the same church, the minister alone always decided what hymns would be sung. A study of church bulletins over the span of a few years revealed that the same cycle of hymns was repeated every twelve months. The congregation came to know and love these eighty to a hundred hymns, but had no knowledge whatsoever of the other four hundred in the hymnal.

It is a good thing for a congregation to sing hymns often enough to know them well. It is also good for worshipers to have favorite hymns or songs and to look forward to their use in worship. It is equally important to look at the range of music used in the worship service and to consider its historical and theological foundations. How decisions are made concerning the selection of music needs to be understood so that it both correctly represents the faith and meets the expectations of the people.

The New Testament records two characteristics of Christian singing: It was filled with the Holy Spirit, and it was the expression of a conscious faith. It was not music for its own sake but a means of expressing the Word of God.[2] These observations might well serve as guidelines for all the music that occurs during Christian worship.

James White, an authority on Christian worship, suggests three basic categories of music one is likely to encounter in Christian worship: (1) *congregational*, or music to be sung or chanted by everyone present in the worship service; (2) *choral*, or music to be sung or chanted by some but not all in the worship service; and (3) *instrumental*, or music that may be accompanied by movement, but not voice.[3]

Congregational Music

White says that congregational song is the most important kind of music in Christian worship.[4] This is in keeping with his belief that the best worship is participatory and interactive rather than passive. Both visitors and regular worshipers are more likely to join in if the hymns are familiar, easy to sing, and favorites of the congregation. It is particularly important that the first hymn be one which the congregation can sing well. The visitor will be impressed by the degree of enthusiasm with which the regulars sing, and church members will more likely participate with enthusiasm in the rest of the service if the first thing they are invited to do is sing something they enjoy.

Congregational singing has long been a part of Christian worship. The New Testament has many references to congregational singing: Jesus and the disciples singing a hymn in the upper room, after the Passover meal; Paul and Silas singing hymns in the Philippian jail; the admonition in Colossians 3 to "sing psalms and hymns and spiritual songs with thankfulness to God;" and the multitudes singing praise to God in the Revelation to John. Congregational song was a way of learning scripture, of praying, of reciting creeds (as in Phil. 2:5–11), of encouraging fellow worshipers and of exalting God's name. Singing has been a part of reform and renewal movements. Perhaps the most famous example is Charles Wesley, without whom the Methodist movement would not have gotten far. In more recent history, well-known teams of preacher and musician/songleader have been Dwight L. Moody and Ira Sankey, Billy Sunday and Homer Rodeheaver, and Billy Graham and George Beverly Shea.

The reasons church members are so strongly invested in congregational music are that it shapes and reinforces their faith—more so, perhaps, than any other part of worship in which they participate. When new denominational hymnals are published, or a new pastor comes to a church, an assessment is made of the kind of faith and religious experience fostered in a congregation or denomination by the music being sung. The same kind of assessment may be made by the church's worship committee or music committee. A frame of reference for considering congregational music is needed in order to carry out the task in a way that is fair and intelligible to all.

For example, although most Christians can tell whether they are in an Episcopal or Baptist church by the music being sung, they may have a hard time naming those differences. Congregational music may be divided into several kinds of songs, some of which are more popular in a given denomination than in others. They are as follows: *Hymns*, which are metrical poetry set to music, address God or speak about God, are usually trinitarian and fairly formal in style, and are often praise-oriented. *Gospel songs*, which are more informal and individualistic in style, may be narrative testimonies with refrains that are easy for the congregation to remember, and they may be used with evangelistic preaching. *Spirituals*, often from the black church, articulate the needs and concerns of the community that sings them. They often begin with a refrain, and are rich with metaphorical language having political or sociological overtones.[5] *Psalms* are paraphrased directly from the Bible. John Calvin encouraged their use in worship, and singing psalms aids the congregation in learning biblical texts. *Office hymns* are prescribed for a particular service at a set time of day. A good example of an office hymn is "All Praise to Thee, My God, This Night."

It is safe to say that in most Protestant traditions, church members will spend less time debating about office hymns than about the question of how other hymns, psalms, gospel songs, and spirituals are being used in worship. All the kinds of hymns listed address different theological issues, and all are part of the Christian life and deserve a place in worship. Hymns focus our attention on God as objective reality and/or address God as the one being worshiped and praised. Gospel songs give voice to the congregation's experience of God and may serve an evangelistic function. The Psalms have the advantage of being paraphrased directly from the Bible. In memorizing them the congregation learns biblical texts. Spirituals articulate the needs and concerns of the community at worship, and reinforce that sense of community as God is praised or entreated. Spirituals also recognize the contributions of a segment of society that was excluded in the past.

The challenge to pastors, worship committees, and church musicians is to find a balance of these various kinds of congregational music that not only expresses the faith of those who will sing it, but nurtures that faith in a responsible manner. In selecting congregational music for a given service neither snobbery nor mere sentimentalism should cast votes. Nor should the hymns and songs selected pander to a "lowest common denominator" or manipulate church members according to the wishes of the one making selections. The investment of time, money, and energy in new music for congregational singing should aim to lead Christians at worship into a deeper experience of God, and to acknowledge and celebrate the faith that has brought them thus far.

Choral Music

Choral music, as White describes it, is sung by some but not all of the worshipers present. Its roots go back to Old Testament times. Like other parts of worship, it was carried over from Jewish practices to Christian. From the time when monasteries were established, trained choirs chanted portions of scripture and other parts of the service. As music became more complex and sophisticated, singers with greater training were needed for its presentation in worship. Calvin and Luther did not abandon the use of choirs at the time of the Reformation, but instead employed them to lead the congregation in singing new hymns.[6]

Choirs play three similar but distinct roles in Christian worship: proclaiming the Word, performing music too difficult for the congregation to sing, and leading the other worshipers in singing the hymns. However, if we think of the choir's role in the larger context of the church's ministry, it becomes plain that the choir also serves pastoral, educational, and evangelistic functions. New members may find the choir provides the fellowship they desire while also being a task-oriented group whose primary goal is not intimacy. The youth and children's choirs may be a catechetical tool and a means of involving young members in worship. Children's participation may also serve as a point of entry for the choir members' brothers, sisters, and parents.

Good choral music can help offset weak preaching in a worship service. Even a less-than-perfect choral performance can have redemptive value. When asked what prompted one couple to join the church, the woman responded, "It was the choir. They really messed up on the first line of the anthem, and the director just grinned and said, 'Okay, maybe we'd better try that again!' We wanted to be a part of a church where something like that could happen."

The three liturgical roles of a church choir—proclaiming, performing, and leading—are emphasized in varying degrees, depending on the denomination and context in which the worship takes place. When a choir or soloist sings a piece of music that supports or reinforces the spoken Word, choral music serves the function of proclamation. When a cantata or concert is presented in place of scripture readings and sermons, choral music is clearly performance (what is less clear is if it is worship). When specially trained musicians are used to teach an antiphon, hymn, or chorus to the rest of the worshiping community, their leadership role is prominent.

The *location* of choral musicians in worship space suggests what role they have in a local church. In an Akron plan sanctuary, with the choir behind and perhaps a bit above the pulpit, or off to the side yet still in front of the congregation, the role of proclamation is suggested. The music is coming from approximately the same area as where the scripture is read. As the choir sings hymns with the congregation, a sense of intimacy and mutual encouragement may be fostered as the choir faces the congregation, their voices leading those in the pews. The choir may be located in a balcony at the rear of the nave, that is, behind the congregation. This location suggests solidarity with other worshipers as they face liturgical centers and/or the cross. Because they cannot be a visual distraction when above and behind the pews, this location may also facilitate meditation rather than an audience mentality when the choir is presenting special music. Choir members who are seated in a split chancel or elsewhere and leave their seats to stand on the chancel steps to face the congregation when singing look as though they are engaged in performance. When choir members disperse to sit or stand among the congregation and only come together to sing, the teaching role is prominent.

Sometimes choirs and choral music give mixed messages that make church members uncomfortable, even if they have difficulty describing what it is that makes them uneasy. For example, the minister and choir director may emphasize the idea that the choir is assisting in proclamation of the Word. However, the choir members sing in another language, or use a style of music that is hard for listeners to understand. Their body language while singing may suggest a pep rally or talent show. The result is a mixed message with neither function being served. The same occurs if the church's understanding of choral music is that it is to sing *for* the congregation and to offer something beautiful to God in worship, but the choir is under-prepared and consistently chooses the equivalent of the latest advertising jingle. This "addiction to mediocrity," as Franky Schaeffer calls it, is neither an offering nor an inspiration.[7]

A congregation will do well to begin its consideration of choral music not by asking, How can we get music for Amy Grant's latest hit? but by asking itself what the members believe is the true role of choral music in worship. Only when this issue is addressed can church members look responsibly to questions of the personnel who would best fulfill the church's needs, and how much should be budgeted for the church's music ministry.

One parenthetical word about choral music and the church budget: however limited your church's resources for music to enrich the worship service, it is never permissible to photocopy or use other means to avoid paying for an adequate number of copies of copyrighted music. It is also illegal to use "restricted" music without the publisher's permission—for instance, setting religious words to the tune "Edelweiss." Even if you are not caught and prosecuted, it is stealing nonetheless. The fact that the music is used in a worship service does not justify the act. After all, you would not excuse automobile theft if the thief claimed the car would be used for a worthy cause, would you? Publishers will often grant congregations permission to make a limited number of photocopies for one-time use; the key is to write to the publisher well in advance of the proposed date of use.

Instrumental Music

With the exceptions of a few denominations, such as the Church of Christ and some Eastern Orthodox churches, Christian bodies use instrumental music during worship. An organ or piano is used for the prelude and postlude. (There is, however, no reason prelude and postlude cannot be sung as well as played, although this is rarely done.) Instrumental music may also be used for processionals and recessionals, as background music during silent prayer, as offertory music, and during periods of meditation in the service.

The musical instruments used in Christian worship have varied throughout the history of the church, depending on local custom, technology, and the availability of proficient musicians. There is no mention of particular instruments used in worship in the Apostolic period, but we may imagine they inherited musical as well as liturgical tradition from Jewish roots. First Samuel 16:23 describes David playing the lyre to drive the evil spirit from King Saul. In Psalm 150, there is a list of instruments to be used in worshiping God: trumpet, lute, harp, tambourine, strings, pipe, and cymbals. In Revelation, John describes the song of the 144,000 as sounding like harps; various angelic messengers mentioned in that book blow trumpets.

As the church spread across Asia and Europe, instrumental music as well as choral music came to be used for processions and other aspects of worship. From the fourth century onward, instrumental music was used in pilgrimages, weddings, and processions for Rogationtide (special days of prayer on April 25 and the three days preceding Ascension Day). On all occasions when Christians were engaged in liturgical acts outside their place of worship and mixing with non-Christians who could not join in choral or congregational music, instruments were played. Through most of the history of the Western church, the title, purpose, mood, and mental associations of the listeners, rather than the actual structure or melodic progression, have determined the fitness of a piece of music for worship. An example of this is Bach's "Air for the G String," which is commonly played in Christian worship although there is nothing intrinsically religious about it.

A theological concern to be kept in mind when selecting instrumental music is whether it enhances and supports the proclaimed Word that precedes or follows it. It should be in keeping with the season of the church year in which it is to be used, and should not distract those at worship by deliberately evoking mental associations not conducive to worship. For example, a prelude to be played on Good Friday should be more somber and measured than the exuberant and joyous prelude for Easter morning. In most Christian traditions, instrumental music used during silent prayer will be the kind that facilitates a reflective, reverent, listening posture on the part of worshipers, rather than having a lively rhythm that sets the congregation tapping their toes.

A minister or worship committee wishing to enhance the contribution of instrumental music to worship may invite the people in the congregation to submit titles, recordings, and copies of music they find inspirational. These can then be sorted out according to appropriateness, practicality, and occasion or liturgical season. An inventory of musicians in the congregation and their degree of proficiency may enable a higher degree of lay participation in the leadership of worship, particularly if someone in the church can edit and transpose music for the varying degrees of skill among the musicians. Foresight exercised in the physical arrangement of the instrumentalists and the placement of their contributions in the service will minimize the distraction of seeing something new up front. This will help the congregation think of their part in the service as genuine worship rather than a performance.

Music can be one of the most important and meaningful aspects of a service of worship. It is something about which virtually every one has definite opinions. It is of the utmost importance to the people who attend church on Sunday mornings that the music performed and the hymns sung contribute to their experience of worship.

Evaluation of the Music Used in Worship

Assessing Our Situation

The following questions deal with the music used in the worship services in your church. Please answer these the best you can by making a check in the appropriate place.

1. Are different types of music used in the service of worship?

   _____yes   _____uncertain   _____no

2. Do you know what person or group chooses music for worship in your church?

   _____yes   _____uncertain   _____no

3. Do you think most of the worshipers find the hymns meaningful?

   _____yes   _____uncertain   _____no

4. Does the church have a choir that sings regularly?

   _____yes   _____uncertain   _____no

5. Do the congregational hymns generally fit the theme of the service?

   _____yes   _____uncertain   _____no

6. Does the music sung by the choir generally fit the theme of the service?

   _____yes   _____uncertain   _____no

7. Are instruments other than a piano or organ used in the service of worship?

   _____yes   _____uncertain   _____no

8. Is there an effort to enable the congregation to learn new hymns?

   _____yes   _____uncertain   _____no

9. Does the congregation use the denominational book of hymns?

   _____yes   _____uncertain   _____no

10. Is an appropriate amount of money (considering the membership of the church) spent on the music program?

    _____yes   _____uncertain   _____no

Now go back over your answers to the questions and give each a score. Write in the scores in the spaces below. Give each "yes" a score of 3, each "uncertain" a score of 2, and each "no" a score of 1. If you could not answer the question give it a score of 0.

Question	Score
One	_____
Two	_____
Three	_____
Four	_____
Five	_____
Six	_____
Seven	_____
Eight	_____
Nine	_____
Ten	_____
Total	_____

Add the scores. The total may range from 0 (the weakest score) to 30 (the strongest score). How do the scores given by the members of your group compare with each other?

Discussing the Issues

1. In general, how knowledgeable are your group members about the music program in your church?

2. How would you evaluate the music in the worship services?

3. What changes would you like to see made in the music program in your church?

Responding to the Issues

If the scores from the first section were generally weak, your church may have more of a problem with communication than with music per se. Perhaps there are many newcomers to the church in your group or there has been a recent change in church personnel. A weak score also means that it is likely that the group had difficulty addressing the third question for discussion, or that it was used primarily to vent dissatisfaction. If this was the case for you, the group using this book would do well to invite the pastor and/or director of music to give a session explaining the way music is chosen for worship and the philosophy behind the church's music ministry. This will benefit both the pastor and your group. Not only will it facilitate greater ownership of this aspect of worship, but it may also force the pastor to rethink some assumptions about the role of music in church. For instance, if the minister has been using music as "filler" or mere background for what is perceived as the "main event" (usually preaching), your discussion of this chapter can move him or her beyond aesthetics alone to an appreciation of the devotional and catechetical aspects of congregational and choral music.

If there is a strong level of understanding of the church's music program, but equally strong disagreement with it, possible reasons are: (1) individuals or groups are striving for an unhealthy degree of control over this part of worship; (2) the congregation is made up of people with widely divergent theological and musical traditions; (3) there are not adequate opportunities for using a variety of musical and liturgical styles. In the first case, music is a screen for another problem in the church. In the second and third cases, the pastor and laity can work cooperatively to provide expression for the faith-traditions represented in the congregation.

5. The Sermon

The sermon has traditionally been the longest segment of the Sunday worship service in Protestant churches. Many believe it is the most important part. When a congregation considers a prospective pastor, the person's preaching ability is a major factor in the decision. Preaching is particularly important in attracting people to worship and creating a congregational sense of identity in contemporary megachurches. The drawing power of these congregations rests largely on the charisma of the preacher. Effective preaching is often what attracts people under thirty-five, particularly those who are not enculturated, church-going Christians. Preaching also plays a critical role in the creation of new faith communities.

But a case can also be made for saying that preaching is now given less importance than at other times in the church's history. Certainly, if its importance is measured by the amount of time devoted to the task, the significance of preaching appears to have declined. Few church members clamor for longer sermons from their pastor. If the service does not end after one hour, the minister will likely hear complaints. Jonathan Edwards and Phillips Brooks, two famous and highly regarded preachers in American history, would not find much market for their sermons today; they would be criticized for going on altogether too long. Today's preachers also spend less time in sermon preparation than yesterday's "pulpit giants" did. Few clergy can spend fifteen to twenty hours per week formulating their Sunday message.

Instead, the expectation is that he or she will give attention to a wide range of professional and pastoral activities our forebears never imagined.

Yet it is claimed that quality preaching is of crucial importance for the health of the worshiping congregation and the continuity of the church. William Thompson has written:

> Preaching has captured the attention of increasingly large segments of the American public. Lay parish committees seeking pastoral leadership consistently rank preaching as the most desirable pastoral skill. Seminary courses and clergy conferences on preaching attract participants in larger numbers than ever. Millions of viewers watch television preachers every week.[1]

If Thompson is right—and he probably is—how can we explain the frustration many church members experience when they listen to their preacher on Sunday morning? Some frustration is engendered by our culture's changing expectations of the preacher. As Thompson acknowledges, virtually everyone today has been exposed to preachers on radio and television whose appealing delivery cannot be matched by the pastor of the nearby local church. Television preachers may work with teleprompters; congregations come to expect the same sustained eye contact with their pastor. The personal attractiveness and warmth projected by the electronic church preachers cultivate the hope that one's own pastor will be the same. The smooth, flowing delivery possible when one is working in a closed studio is much harder to attain when the preacher is competing with a crying baby in the fourth pew or is worried about going overtime because the choir director insisted on an extra anthem. It should be noted that a third of the largest congregations in America are served by a senior pastor who did not graduate from a theological seminary but who apparently has mastered the skill of effective preaching.

Of course, the frustration worshipers experience when listening to a sermon may be the fault of the preacher. He or she may have bad sermon preparation habits, such as not taking adequate time to prepare, using canned sermon illustrations or borrowed sermons, or riding the same hobbyhorse year after year. And the preacher may react with defensiveness and hostility to constructive criticism about the sermon. He or she may firmly believe that the preaching is just fine, and blame the congregation for unreasonable expectations.

Myths About Preaching

Even if your pastor is doing (or not doing) one or more of the things mentioned above, the people in the pews bear some responsibility for their own frustration. It is unlikely the minister's counterproductive sermon strategies arose from a vacuum. In all probability, your congregation or the last church your pastor served unknowingly reinforced such behavior by believing one or more of the five great myths about preaching. The myths, which have circulated in the churches for many years, have just enough truth in them to make them plausible. They do not create better preaching; they create greater dissatisfaction. They put the preacher and the congregation in an adversarial relationship. Let us look at each of them in turn, and discuss why they do not stand up under scrutiny.

Myth One: We can't get good preachers because they're not teaching them right in the seminaries.

If this were true, creating pulpit giants would simply be a matter of hiring better seminary faculty and using the greatest homiletics textbooks ever written. Experienced teachers of preaching find that in a given class some people will naturally be stronger preachers than others. The late professor Ronald Sleeth used to say that the two kinds of preachers he enjoyed teaching most were the gifted and the disabled, because they presented the greatest challenge. However, most students are somewhere in between these two. Seminary classes will always have students with a mix of talent and ability. Myth one is incorrect because right teaching cannot guarantee that every seminary graduate will be a great preacher on Sunday morning.

A congregation would be wise to learn more about the seminary from which its clergy come. What course(s) in preaching are required for graduation? Is the teaching of preaching taken seriously? Are students required to take any Bible or theology courses before they take preaching? Are continuing education courses in preaching offered to pastors? What preaching courses do your denomination or judicatory require of candidates for ministry? The seminary cannot teach students if they are not in classes in preaching.

Myth Two: All denominations ought to have some system of trial sermons or neutral pulpits so the congregation can make a better informed decision as to whether they want a given preacher.

Some denominations require a prospective pastor to preach for them so they can judge whether they like his or her theology and style. This may happen in the church with the opening, or a pulpit committee may arrange to visit the church served by the candidate. An advantage of the trial sermon is that it does separate the good or adequate preacher from the inept one. The pulpit committee may come to grips with its own theology of preaching in the process of considering a candidate. A fairer, more accurate assessment is made when people see and hear someone preach than when they make a decision based on a manuscript, or on hearsay, in which opinion about the candidate's preaching skills may be confused with other pastoral skills or personality. In some denominations, such as the United Methodist, a bishop appoints the pastor to a church so the congregation does not hear him or her preach in advance.

What is mythological about trial sermons making better preachers? It is that no one sermon can do everything. It cannot indicate the long-term effectiveness of the pastor-congregation relationship. It is impossible to tell how good a match will be on the basis of one twenty-minute message, especially if it is preached in a context unfamiliar to the preacher or the committee. A trial sermon is the ecclesiastical equivalent of a blind date! When young people fall in love at first sight, it is called infatuation and not expected to last. It is only when two parties have known each other awhile that they can appreciate one another's deeper qualities and communicate more effectively.

There is also a theological problem inherent in trial sermons. If the purpose is to grade the performance, those holding the scorecards are not really worshiping. If the minister understands he or she must perform impressively in the pulpit that Sunday in order to get a better job, the witness to the gospel may be compromised. The preacher may be striving to please humans rather than God. The people in the pews and pulpit are less open to the work of the Holy Spirit in worship when they're busy sizing one another up.

Myth Three: The best way to increase attendance at worship is to get a better preacher. We'll keep saying no to the bishop or to candidates until we get the preacher we want.

This is a half-truth. People attend a particular church for a variety of complex reasons. Preaching is an important motivating factor, but by no means the only one. However, the worship service is usually a visitor's first encounter with a church, and impressions received influence the individual's decision to return. The sermon is part of that first impression. Therefore, good preaching may be an incentive for visitors to return; poor preaching may repel them.

Two additional factors further deflate the myth. First, people in a highly mobile society attending your congregation for the first time are probably there because the location and hour were convenient, or a friend invited them. The visitors on Sunday morning may be from several denominations, each of which has its own worship and preaching traditions. People have differing and sometimes unconscious expectations of what constitutes good preaching, so that "better" becomes a relative issue.

Second, if good preaching were the prime consideration in church attendance, we might expect that most of the church-going population in a given community would spend Sunday morning listening to the area pulpit star. Why should they go somewhere else and settle for second best? The reason they do is that other aspects of worship and congregational life play an important role in church attendance. In a small congregation, fellowship, loyalty, and other factors may make up for deficiencies in the pulpit. The larger the congregation, the more significant the sermon is likely to

be to newcomers shopping for a church. In large congregations they are not as likely to have the Word mediated to
them through personal encounters with other worshipers.
One might conclude that although a correlation can be made
between the significance of the sermon to the overall worship experience and the size of the congregation, preaching
is only one of several motivations for regular attendance.

Myth Four: If only we could get a preacher like (fill in
name, perhaps a former pastor), everybody would be happy.

This is closely related to Myth Three. It cannot be true, because it is impossible to find a preacher who (1) will be an
exact clone of anyone else, or (2) can meet everyone's expectations. Chances are that the memories of a former pastor or
partial knowledge of another preacher are romanticized and
unrealistic. A friend used to quip, "Show me a perfect church
and I'll show you a church you don't know!" The same re-
mark can be made about those who lead worship.

Consider the personalities and needs of the people in
your household or in the group reading this book together.
Are your emotional and spiritual needs identical to those of
the person next to you? A young child may need the
preacher to embody the warmth and accessibility of God.
The teenager needs a spiritual leader who will help that
teenager develop his or her own identity and accountability
to God and to himself or herself. The single adult may need
a preacher who leads the congregation in being the family of
God. The parents of school-aged children may want a
preacher who will speak to the pressures on the Christian
family today. Each individual's hopes and needs change
from one period of life to another. These needs are all legitimate. A gifted preacher will fashion the sermon so that many
listeners will feel the message was prepared especially for
them. However, no one preacher can address all those needs
in depth in the same sermon. An exit poll would be likely to
reveal that those whose needs were not addressed directly
are also less satisfied with the preacher and the sermon.

Myth Five: Preaching is a solo act. That's why we pay the
pastors' salaries. They ought to deliver what they're hired
to do.

Preaching is a solo act in that usually only one person speaks, but in many ways we may think of it as a corporate act of worship. Many conversations are going on during the sermon. The Word of God we call the Bible addresses the preacher in sermon preparation and continues to address preacher and listeners in the worship service. During the sermon, the preacher responds to that Word and interprets it with and for the congregation. The experiences, hopes, and struggles of the congregation interact with the spoken word, the living Word, and with each other. The lives of men and women of faith who are part of the worshipers' memories influence the way the preacher's words are heard. The Holy Spirit works in all of these processes, so that a given preaching event may evoke new knowledge of God's truth, repentance of sins, awareness of grace, reconciliation with others, or resolution to pursue a particular course of action. This is a far cry from simply passive listening.

Even the composition of sermons is not a solo act. The preacher makes use of biblical commentaries written by others. Events in the life of the congregation the previous week may shape the direction of the message, even if they are not mentioned explicitly. The prayers of the congregation for the pastor's preaching, the number of telephone calls during sermon preparation, and other events in the life of the church may find conscious or unconscious expression in the Sunday sermon.

If the five great myths are not adequate for assessing what happens in the pulpit Sunday morning, what tools does a congregation have for understanding what is happening during the sermon? How can the listeners be helped in formulating suggestions for what should happen?

Components of Preaching

In "Preaching as Confluence,"[2] Conrad Massa describes preaching as the coming together of four distinct components. Without all four components one may have a sermon manuscript, but one does not have preaching. Several analytical questions may be asked about the preaching in your

church by using Massa's framework. Discussing these questions may help you better understand the components of
preaching.

The first component is the *preacher*. This may strike people as obvious, but chances are they do not appreciate the
significance of the messenger in their apprehension of the
message. Communications experts tell us that up to 90 per-
cent of our communication is nonverbal. We evaluate what
we hear largely on the basis of our response to something
other than the words being spoken. Furthermore, the
English language has a redundancy rate of around 50 per-
cent. This is to say that we can usually understand what another person is saying even if half the words in the sentence
are omitted. The preacher's physical appearance, choice of
dress, hairstyle, and way of standing all convey something
to the hearers before he or she says anything beyond "Let us
pray." The preacher's gestures, pitch of voice, regional ac-
cent, use of colloquial expressions, length and quality of eye
contact, pace at which words are spoken, and projected atti-
tudes all contribute to what is communicated to the hearers.

A congregation would do well to ask the following questions: What is the predominant mood or attitude of the
preacher? Is it reverent or perfunctory, formal or casual, aloof
or friendly? Does he or she look relaxed or tense? When
preaching, does this person relate to the congregation primarily as a parental figure, a priest, a prophet, a good
buddy, or something else? What self-understanding and assumptions about the congregation does the preacher project
during the sermon? What does our congregation believe and
value about the person and role of a preacher?

After a minister's first Sunday in a new church, one of the
leaders of the congregation said he thought things went all
right but that the pastor came across as aloof and formal. He
was asked to tell in what ways he saw this expressed, how
he thought the congregation reacted to it, and how the minister's manner compared with that of the previous pastor.
He responded that the previous minister never preached
from the pulpit, but walked up and down the center aisle,
and that he rarely wore a robe.

The congregation did not ask that the style of the previous pastor be mimicked, but they let their new minister know about the contrast between the two. Ways that the pastor could communicate with the warmth and informality they valued were discussed. What the congregation truly longed for was not one particular person rather than another; they expected that the grace and reconciling nature of God be communicated and they knew this could be done in more than one way.

The second component framework is the *listeners*. Congregations should do a "reality check" to determine if they are who they believe they are, and are who the preacher believes they are. Do they see themselves as pillars of the church? Is the congregation stable or mobile? Do the sermons address the congregation as though they were one kind of people (families with young children, for instance) when in fact they are another kind (older adults)? Does the preacher speak to them as though they are deeply invested in the Christian faith and the life of that congregation, or as casual visitors? Does the preacher seem to know or care what questions they have about the nature of God and how to live faithfully?

One congregation wished their preacher would have altar calls at the end of the sermon so that people could go forward and receive Christ. They cherished the beliefs that (1) people should be converted during preaching and (2) their worship ought to be aimed at converting souls. However, a look around the sanctuary revealed that virtually everyone present had been a church member for years. Many had undergone conversion experiences in their youth. They wanted sermons aimed at the unconverted, even though they counted themselves as among the converted. The preacher and the congregation were generally frustrated, though for different reasons.

One might ask what clues the preacher gives as to his or her expectations of the congregation, and whether the congregation concurs. For instance, if the preacher prints the sermon outline in the bulletin and designates space in the bulletin for note-taking, he or she is communicating one or more of the following: (1) that the congregation will not understand the complex theological ideas being offered so a study guide is necessary; (2) that they will not want to miss a single thought of this terrific sermon; (3) that the congregation will want to discuss or meditate on the sermon later on; (4) that they can be sure the pastor devoted much time to sermon preparation. What other things might be communicated by an outline or space for notes? How would your congregation respond to these unspoken messages?

The third component in preaching is what is said, that is, the *sermon content*. Careful listening to someone's sermons over time should enable anyone to answer the following questions: Who is Jesus Christ for this preacher? What are the essentials of the Christian faith? What authority does scripture have in these messages? What other authorities can be identified? How is scripture used in sermons? Is what the preacher says theologically coherent? Does it make sense given what was said last Sunday, or what is being talked about in Sunday school, or what is happening in the rest of the worship service?

Most congregations believe preaching should be biblical, but the relationship between text and sermon may be expressed in many different ways. A sermon may explore a passage in the Bible carefully and in depth. It may sum up the theme of a passage and then discuss the theme. The sermon may not be based on a *single* text but instead may be a more topical message that makes reference to many passages in the Bible. The sermon may impress listeners as being generally Christian or religious but not be based on any text. The sermon may be contradictory to the generally accepted understanding of the text. Your denomination or local congregation will have expectations concerning the right way(s) of understanding and interpreting the Bible in preaching. Most congregations learn to listen to an exposition of a text in a certain way. Among some ethnic minorities, for example, the preacher is expected to spend a long time working through the scripture reading for the day verse by verse, before making any connections with the lives of the listeners.

Another question to be asked about sermon content is whether the preacher is following the lectionary and, if so, which one. A lectionary is a yearly schedule of suggested readings taken from the Old Testament, the Gospels, and other books of the New Testament. Such schedules of readings from the Hebrew Bible were used in synagogue worship in Jesus' day. The early church quickly formulated its own lectionaries. A preacher may employ the ecumenical Common Lectionary, which is used by many denominations, or devise his or her own plan of readings for several Sundays based on a theme or document (such as the Apostles' Creed or the Ten Commandments) or on a current congregational concern. Arguments in favor of the lectionary are that it acquaints the congregation with more of scripture than they might otherwise hear in worship. It minimizes the possibility that a preacher will stick with a few pet topics or biblical books. It fosters unity with churches of other denominations using the same lectionary. Arguments against the lectionary are that, when rigidly enforced, it may stifle the leading of the Holy Spirit in the preacher and congregation. An editorial board formulating a lectionary always operates with biases (sometimes unconscious) in text selections. Lectionary readings may not be sensitive to the needs and issues of a particular congregation at a particular time. The preacher may try to force a connection among the texts of the day where no connection exists. Your congregation may have expectations concerning the use or non-use of a lectionary in preaching.

Questions may be asked about the way the preacher develops ideas in a sermon. Is there a regular pattern in the sermons, such as three points and a poem? Does the sermon always start with a funny story? Does it always contain a story about what happened to the preacher that week? What picture of the world is presented in the sermons? Is it a fair and accurate description? Are there certain phrases, ideas, or persons who appear with great regularity in the sermons? For example, in the sermons by one preacher the rich young ruler, the woman at the well, Zacchaeus, or the prodigal son made an appearance every Sunday—no matter what the text or topic was.

And what does the sermon *do*? Among the most important questions that can be asked about a sermon are, "Why did this word need to be spoken and heard?" and "How would you summarize, in one sentence, what the preacher was trying to communicate?" If few in the congregation can answer these questions, there has been a breakdown in communication. If the preacher cannot answer them, something is even more seriously wrong.

The final component is the *context:* the relationship of what is said in the sermon and the way it is said to the rest of the worship service, to the things the preacher and other people do in worship, to the total program of the church, and to the setting in which it all takes place. The placement of the sermon in the larger service suggests something about context. If, for example, the only thing after the sermon is a closing hymn, the understanding being communicated is that preaching is the climax toward which the rest of worship has been building. One may respond to an invitation given from the pulpit during or after the service, but it will be an individual response rather than something the worshiping community does together. The context of the sermon may suggest that the community may respond to the proclaimed Word in a number of ways. These can include sharing joys and sorrows, praying for others, giving testimony to how the Word has spoken to an individual in the congregation, presenting offerings to God, and singing praise.

A consideration of context will also draw our attention to the appropriateness of a given sermon to the time and place it is preached. The same content will be heard (and probably said) one way in an Episcopal church and another way in a Baptist church. This is because the traditions of these two denominations have different ways of shaping the material in a message and acknowledging the worship style in which the sermon is uttered. A canned sermon, or one from the minister's barrel, betrays itself because it does not take the time and place in which it is preached seriously. This is evident not only in illustrations used but also in the choice of vocabulary and the preacher-listener relationship that is projected.

While preaching will continue to be the longest section of the Sunday service, and very important to those at worship when they decide whether to return the next Sunday, it is likely the style and structure of Christian preaching will continue to change. After all, sermon manuscripts from the seventh century do not read (or sound) like those from the eleventh, eighteenth, or twentieth. Literary styles, oral communication, and theological emphases evolve over time.

The sermons that have stood the test of time and continue to be studied in our own day are not necessarily those whose pastoral and prophetic concerns are timeless and whose illustrations could be drawn from any century. Nor are they the sermons by men and women regarded as great leaders of the church in other respects. The best sermons of previous ages and our own are those whose content reveals that the speaker was compelled to preach by the power of God, whose words illuminate and bear witness to the Word. Their transparency, even when the style is fumbling and not particularly articulate, reveals the grace and majesty of the Lord people have come seeking to know and to worship.

Evaluation of the Sermon

Assessing Our Situation

The following items deal with your understanding of preaching in your denomination and in the church where you worship. Please answer these the best you can by making a check in the appropriate box.

1. Does the preaching in this church impress you as typical of your denomination?
   _____yes   _____uncertain   _____no
2. Does the minister schedule a certain block of time each week for sermon preparation, and do members respect that schedule?
   _____yes   _____uncertain   _____no
3. Does the church budget earmark funds for use for the minister to attend continuing education events in preaching and other subjects?
   _____yes   _____uncertain   _____no

4. Is the relationship between the sermon and the scripture reading clear?

    _____yes   _____uncertain   _____no

5. Do the sermons preached in this church speak to the lives of those who worship here?

    _____yes   _____uncertain   _____no

6. Can you usually follow what the preacher is saying, and is the point of the sermon intelligible?

    _____yes   _____uncertain   _____no

7. Is the preacher's nonverbal communication (in dress or general appearance, gestures, and so on) harmonious with sermon content?

    _____yes   _____uncertain   _____no

8. Does the preacher speak with conviction and a sense of the importance of his or her message for the congregation?

    _____yes   _____uncertain   _____no

9. Is the delivery of the sermon appropriate to the subject matter?

    _____yes   _____uncertain   _____no

10. Do the illustrations seem about the right length, and do they fit the subject of the sermon?

    _____yes   _____uncertain   _____no

11. Is the congregation's overall response to preaching here positive?

    _____yes   _____uncertain   _____no

12. Does the sermon fit with the rest of the worship service?

    _____yes   _____uncertain   _____no

Now go back over your answers to the questions and give each a score. Write in the scores in the spaces below. Give each "yes" a score of 3, each "uncertain" a score of 2, and each "no" a score of 1. If you could not answer the question give it a score of 0.

Question	Score
One	_____
Two	_____
Three	_____
Four	_____

Five   _____
Six   _____
Seven   _____
Eight   _____
Nine   _____
Ten   _____
Eleven   _____
Twelve   _____

Total   _____

Add the scores. The totals may range from 0 (the weakest score) to 36 (the strongest score). How do the scores given by the members of your group compare with each other?

Discussing the Issues

1. Is there any consensus in the group as to what is valued as good preaching? Can you identify the qualities of this preaching as well as the person who does it?

2. Have any group members offered specific comments to the minister about a sermon (more than "good message" or "that spoke to me")? How were these comments received?

3. Does your pastor have regular opportunities to hear other preachers besides those on television and radio?

Responding to the Issues

One strategy I use in introductory preaching classes is try to identify at least one aspect of the preacher's work that was praiseworthy, and draw the preacher's attention to it. Members of your group can improve the preaching at your church by using a similar method. This is not to deny whatever shortcomings your preacher may have but to encourage the pastor to build on his or her strengths. It requires practiced listening skills on Sunday morning, but the rewards benefit the entire congregation.

Another way to facilitate better preaching is to urge the pastor to take continuing education courses in preaching and related subjects. Your denomination may in fact require some continuing education for its clergy, and even provide partial funding. Writing to the nearest theological schools is a source of information about such courses.

6. The Liturgy

Liturgy is the word which has come to describe the order of the worship service. Strictly speaking, the word liturgy denotes the Eucharist; some traditions use the word as a synonym for Holy Communion.[1] In other Christian circles, the word liturgy is not used because the idea of a fixed order of service seems contrary to the free movement of the Holy Spirit in worship. To some, the idea of liturgy seems mysterious, something for ordained clergy rather than laity. The focus of this chapter will be on the Liturgy of the Word, that is, the various parts of the worship as they may be identified in a worship bulletin most Sundays. There will be a brief discussion of differences between a Eucharistic and non-Eucharistic Sunday service and where those differences are manifested.

Three major questions concerning liturgy to be addressed in the pages that follow are: (1) Where did our church get the liturgy and form of worship now being used? (2) What do the various parts of the liturgy mean? (3) What is "good" liturgy for our church?

Where Did Our Church Get Its Present Liturgy?

Christians have always followed a pattern in their worship. Though there were variations in local custom, the usual worship service included reading of the scriptures, preaching, several kinds of prayers, singing, and the sacrament of Holy Communion. (In the earliest times, baptism of converts was done at the Easter vigil and other special periods rather than being added to the Sunday service.) Different kinds of prayers were said at different points in the service. We do not expect to hear the benediction at the beginning of the worship service, and we would be very surprised to hear the minister say, "Now I lay me down to sleep . . . " at the end of the sermon. Most Christian groups have inherited some such rudimentary structure of the liturgy.

The denomination of which you are a part may suggest or mandate a certain order of service. If, for example, you are part of an evangelical tradition with a history of camp-meetings and revivals, chances are good that the sermon is the climax of the worship service. Only a hymn and an invitation to make a commitment to Christ may follow. If you are preaching for conversions and plan to have an altar call, the worship service can lose its momentum if there are many other acts of worship between sermon and invitation. If, on the other hand, your church traces its worship style to the Reformation period, the service may not revolve quite so much around the sermon (though the sermon is quite important). When the Eucharist is not celebrated, there will nonetheless be prescribed acts of worship that follow the sermon. In addition to the order of service, your denomination may have a collection of worship materials which your church may or must use. It may teach you to call various parts of the liturgy by certain names not used by the church down the street. What you call "the bread and the cup" your neighbors may know as "the elements," "the emblems," or "the body and blood."

Some aspects of the worship service used in your church may have had their origins in the ecumenical movement of the twentieth century. As Christians from different traditions have met together for worship, from the local community Thanksgiving Day service to the World Council of Churches' Faith and Order Commission, there has been greater awareness of the extent to which beliefs and practices are shared and the way one tradition or culture may enrich or challenge another. Evidence of ecumenism in the worship at your church may be the use of prayers or hymns that you recognize as coming from another tradition; the introduction of something new into the liturgy, such as a different kind of bread in the Eucharist, or receiving the Eucharist in a way you have not done before; or praying for people and concerns that have not always been a part of your intercessions.

Another source of worship practices is what is referred to as liturgical renewal. Some clergy and laity are paying attention to new worship materials being published and considering whether those materials would work in their churches. There is a shift away from worship oriented primarily toward the ear to worship that involves the entire body. For instance, during Holy Week a preacher may speak about Jesus' washing the disciples' feet, but in recent years an actual footwashing may be incorporated into the same service. This ritual is in fact a very old one, going back to at least the seventh century. Footwashing services are nothing new in some traditions, such as the Mennonites and Seventh-day Adventists. However, the ritual is less familiar in mainline denominations. People may have read about it, but few have seen it done. When introducing an unfamiliar liturgical act, the worship leader may give preliminary words to minimize congregational anxiety about what will happen. The bulletin may include prayers or other words for the congregation to say at a prescribed moment in the service.

A particular act of worship or the entire order of service may be the result of a personal idiosyncrasy of the pastor, congregation, or both. A visitor to the church may or may not notice the individuality of the congregation's worship style, depending on how congruent the act or symbol seems with the rest of worship. In one church bulletin, under the rubric "Prayers of Concern," there was a lengthy paragraph of intercession for a variety of concerns, which continued with the following: "Now dear Lord, we ask a special consideration be given to those who are dear to us in their time of need. Ray Anderson; George, Marie, and Ellen Carlson; Violet, Jean, and Martha; and Kay . . . ." Any visitor would conclude correctly that this prayer, as a fixed part of the liturgy, finds its origins in the individual pastor, worship committee, or congregation. The names might change from week to week, but the fact that the names of several individuals and families are printed is clearly a decision of whomever planned that service.

There is, of course, always the possibility that no one knows why a certain saying, act, or symbol is part of the liturgy. It was incorporated so long ago that no one remembers the reason. When this is the case, a new meaning may be assigned to the act or symbol which can enhance or trivialize that part of worship. A lifelong church member approached the pastor after a eucharistic service on Pentecost, and said, "I love that red stole with the white robe. It's so fitting for Holy Communion—red and white: the Body and the Blood." In this case, re-investing the symbol with meaning added to the member's participation in worship. In another church, most in the congregation believed that the "IHS" on the cross stood for "In His Service" rather than being the first three letters in the Greek word for Jesus. Though a small mistake in itself, such a belief can subtly shift the focus of a worship service from the One who was on the cross to the worshipers' contemplation of what they think they have done in Jesus' service.

What Do the Various Parts of the Liturgy Mean?

Whether one is in a suburban Episcopal church or an inner-city Pentecostal service, the Sunday morning service in North American Protestant churches nearly always follows some variation of this basic pattern of liturgy: an entrance rite, proclamation, response, and sending forth.

When Holy Communion is part of the Sunday morning service, it will occur after the proclamation. Depending on the theology and practice of the church, communion may be understood to be part of the response to the Word proclaimed, or it may be a separate section of the liturgy, "Thanksgiving and Communion." In some traditions, baptism of converts will take place during the "response" portion of the service, following an invitation to faith by the pastor.

One of the most frustrating experiences for Christians at worship (clergy and laity alike) is being confronted with an unfamiliar or uncomfortable portion of liturgy, asking why it is part of the worship service, and getting a definition rather than an explanation. What follows is an attempt to answer some of the "why" questions as well as the "what" questions. These acts of worship are described more or less in the order in which they occur in *The United Methodist Hymnal* (1989), but may vary from one denomination to another.[2]

An Entrance Rite

This may include choral, congregational, and/or instrumental music, opening words, prayers of various kinds, and greetings.

Prelude and/or Gathering. A musical prelude is the introduction to the main theme of the worship service. It introduces people to the purpose for which they gather, and provides a transition from other activities to the corporate worship of God. For this reason a prelude is normally quiet, contemplative music that enables the worshiper to meditate and pray rather than being a showy, dramatic piece that draws attention to the talent of the musician or composer. After the prelude, or in place of it, is the gathering, a time when there may be announcements, conversations and fellowship, prayer requests, and the greeting of visitors. This is frequently done at this point so as not to disrupt the flow of acts of worship that follow.

Introit. In the early Western church, the introit was "moving music," a psalm sung by choir and/or congregation during the entrance of the clergy.[3] Ironically, when an introit is sung today, it is not necessarily a psalm, and no one moves! Instead, the introit reinforces the spoken greeting or opening sentence that follows it, and may be a signal that a processional hymn will follow. The introit and call to worship begin the entrance rite. The congregation is making the transition from individual meditation and prayer during the prelude to corporate worship of God. Even if the worship leaders do not make a formal entrance, the gathered community of faith is entering into God's presence. Reverence and joyful adoration are the dominant moods communicated in this portion of the service.

Greeting/Opening Sentences/Call to Worship. These are the first spoken words in the worship service proper. The nature of the words may change from one season of the Christian year to another. The words may hint at the theme of the service that Sunday. The call to worship may be as simple as "Let us worship God," or it may be several sentences long. Whether these words are said by one person or responsively by many, they should announce God's presence in the midst of the congregation and direct people to reverence and praise.

Hymn of Praise. The Sunday morning service is a unique event in the lives of those present. Because it is probably the only time the entire church gathers as a body for the purpose of worshiping God (as opposed to attending to business matters or engaging in service projects), it is appropriate that the first hymn focus attention on the One in whose name people gather, praising God's goodness, power, and mercy. It is also appropriate that, whenever possible, the hymn reflect corporate rather than private worship of God. Therefore, "Joyful, Joyful, We Adore Thee" is a better choice than "Do, Lord, Remember Me" as an opening hymn of praise.

Prayer of the Day/Invocation/Collect, and/or Confession and Pardon, and/or Litany. The first three terms are often used interchangeably, although they are not different names for the same act. To add to confusion, the prayer of the day is likely to be a collect that is likely to be an invocation. A "prayer of the day" is a brief prayer near the beginning of the service. Its content is determined by the liturgical season or theme of the worship service. The prayer may follow "collect" form, which has five distinct parts: the address (such as "Almighty God"), a relative clause ("unto whom all hearts are open"), a petition ("cleanse the thoughts of our hearts"), a result clause ("that we may perfectly love thee"), and a closing doxology ("through Jesus Christ our Lord"). An invocation "invokes" the Holy Spirit, that is, it prays for God's Spirit to be upon the worship service. It may or may not follow collect form, but, like a collect, it is brief. It makes sense for the congregation to pray for the infilling of the Holy Spirit as corporate worship begins.

Sometimes a corporate prayer of confession is said at this point, and, if so, it is followed by words assuring the congregation of God's mercy, or, in some traditions, words of absolution said by the priest. The prayer of confession or prayer of the day may be litanies. These are prayers in which fixed responses are made by the people to short petitions made by the worship leader.[4] General, corporate confessions are found in biblical accounts of worship and in most Christian liturgies.

Act of Praise/Anthem/Gloria in Excelsis. This part of the liturgy, which is considered optional in many denominations and local churches, closes the entrance portion of the service. If choral music is presented, it is often praise-oriented. The Gloria in Excelsis ("Glory to God in the Highest") is not often sung in many mainline denominations in the United States, except occasionally as part of the eucharistic liturgy. Instead, the briefer "Gloria Patri" ("Glory Be to the Father") is sung here or after the psalm. In earlier centuries, however, the Gloria in Excelsis was a regular part of the entrance rite.

Proclamation

The worship service now proceeds to the second movement: proclamation. It is based on the assumption that in worship God and the worshipers interact, and God speaks to the congregation as the Word is read and proclaimed. One or more selections from the Bible are read, and there may be psalms or anthems, preaching, and exhortation.

Scripture Lesson. In some churches, a prayer for illumination is said before the first lesson. Unless the sermon is based on an Old Testament text, the first reading is usually from that part of the Bible. Hearing lessons from the Old Testament, the Gospels, and the rest of the New Testament makes the congregation more familiar with the Bible. If a lectionary is followed, there may be a common theme to all the lessons for a given Sunday.

Psalm. The Psalms were the hymn/prayerbook of the synagogue in ancient Israel, and were chanted by the early
Christian church, too. In many Protestant churches, a responsive reading is used instead of a Psalm as such. However,
many responsive readings are taken from the book of Psalms.
The psalm/reading may be arranged in a variety of ways
(read by one person, read responsively, chanted, sung as a
hymn) depending on the inclination and skill of those participating.

Scripture Lesson. The second lesson, if there is one, is normally from a New Testament book other than the four
Gospels.

Hymn or Song. The second occasion for congregational
singing may echo a theme introduced in the lessons, or may
pertain to the sermon topic, remind worshipers of the season
in the Christian year, simply be a favorite in that church, or
be a new hymn. If this last is the case, the choir or instrumentalists will frequently introduce the tune by using it in
an earlier part of the service, such as the prelude.

Gospel Lesson. Occasionally, if the sermon is based on a
text other than the Gospel reading, the order of the lessons
will be changed. Some churches attach a great ceremony to
the reading of the Gospel, with a procession to the center of
the congregational space, acolytes, special gestures, and the
use of an elaborate, hammered metal Gospel book cover.
More commonly, the congregation will stand during the
Gospel reading, as a sign of reverence for the Savior's
words. In still other churches, only one lesson is read during
a Sunday morning service, and only the reader stands.

Sermon. See chapter 5 for a discussion of the sermon and
its relationship to the liturgy. Having heard the Word read
and interpreted through various media, the proclamation
phase of worship concludes.

Response

The response may take the form of an invitation to
Christian discipleship, the saying of a creed, the presentation
of tithes and offerings, prayers of thanksgiving and interces-

sion, personal testimony, the exercising of charismatic gifts, and/or congregational singing.

Response to the Word. Just as there may be many appropriate answers to an open-ended question, there are many possible responses to proclamation: creed, hymn of invitation, baptism, confirmation, reception of members, exhortation, or testimony. Some are more individual than corporate, but all take place in worship.

This long list is not a miscellaneous catalog of worship acts, though it may look like one. All these acts are based on the premise that the Holy Spirit works within the individual and congregation through the proclamation of the Word, turning persons toward God. In more evangelical denominations, an exhortation or testimony by someone other than the preacher may drive home the message or bear witness to its truth.

In other denominations, a hymn that underscores Jesus' call to discipleship may be sung. The preacher may invite those who wish to make or renew their covenant with God to be baptized or received into membership.

In some cases, but particularly if there is confirmation or reception of members, the candidates or entire congregation may be asked to reaffirm their faith in Christ by a basic confession, such as "Jesus is Lord," or by reciting one of the historic creeds of the church.

In charismatic and Pentecostal traditions, exercising the gifts of the Spirit, such as healing and speaking in tongues, may occur at this time. This may also happen in the next segment of the liturgy, the prayer for others.

Concerns and Prayer/Pastoral Prayer. If prayer concerns were not noted during a gathering at the beginning of the service, that action may occur at this point. In many traditions, this prayer is the longest one in the service, and it is extemporaneous prayer by the pastor. In other denominations, prayer requests may be printed in the bulletin and alluded to only in a general way. It may include thanksgiving and personal petitions. In some denominations, a printed or responsive prayer may be used. The minister may kneel and face the cross during this prayer, even if this is not done during other prayers in the service.

Confession and Pardon. If this is a eucharistic service and no prayer of confession was said earlier, this is where it is likely to occur. Because Jesus said, "this is my blood of the new covenant, poured out for you and for many for the forgiveness of sins," Christians have always confessed their sins before coming to the Lord's table.

The Peace. This controversial portion of the liturgy is also one of the least understood. In the early church, the kiss of peace was a formal and solemn act, accompanied by the words "Peace be with you," and the response, "And with thy spirit." It was regarded as a seal of prayer. The kiss of peace preceded the Eucharist or was the concluding act in the baptismal rite. Unfortunately, in many churches it has degenerated into a general visiting time with no liturgical significance. Newcomers as well as some members are put off by what sometimes appears to be contrived intimacy.

The Offering. The gifts of the congregation are collected and brought forward. These represent the worshipers' response to God's grace as revealed through the Spirit in worship. "Praise God from Whom All Blessings Flow" (commonly called the Doxology) or another hymn may be sung. In some traditions, if Holy Communion is being celebrated, the bread and wine are also brought forward at this time.

With Communion	or	*Without Communion*
Taking the Bread and Cup		Prayer of Thanksgiving, concluding with the
Great Thanksgiving		Lord's Prayer
Breaking the Bread		
Giving the Bread and Cup		

Although it is beyond the scope of this chapter to give a lengthy discussion of eucharistic theology and practice for every mainline denomination in the United States, the four acts in the sequence noted above in the first column are features of nearly every Protestant tradition. The taking of the bread and cup may be merely uncovering them on the table. The Great Thanksgiving, the long prayer said by the minister during the Eucharist, may contain many different parts which have technical names we need not get into here. It will *always* include the Words of Institution, that is, the narrative containing Jesus' words at the Last Supper, as recorded in the Gospels or in First Corinthians. During or following the Great Thanksgiving, the bread may be lifted up, broken in front of the people, or broken in the sense that the minister announces it is given for all. The giving of the bread and cup is the final "indispensable" act in Holy Communion; the means of distribution may vary according to denomination or local custom. Your pastor or literature from your denomination can tell you if your church specifies the kind of bread to be used, whether wine or unfermented grape juice is to be used in Holy Communion, and whether it is customary for the congregation to sing hymns or meditate silently during communion.

If the Eucharist is not part of the service, the person receiving the offering usually says a prayer of thanksgiving and/or dedication. If the Lord's Prayer was not recited at the conclusion of the pastoral prayer, it is said now. In either case it is followed by a hymn or song.

Sending Forth

This may include a hymn (recessional or otherwise), a benediction or other prayer giving a sense of closure to the service, a choral or instrumental response, moments of silence, and/or a postlude.

Hymn or Song. The congregation now makes the transition to the last of the four phases of corporate worship: the sending forth. It can be argued that this last hymn is part of the response rather than the closing rite, and, depending on the lyrics, it may be one or the other. Most Protestants recognize the final hymn as a signal that the service is nearly over, and expect that the music as well as the pastor's words will move toward closure and commissioning for the week ahead. The hymn may be one of commitment, dismissal, reminder of the sermon topic or season in the Christian year, or, especially if it follows communion, it may be a single verse of a hymn or song pertaining to the meal just eaten.

Dismissal/Benediction/Blessing. An example of dismissal is, "The Mass is ended; go in peace." A benediction or blessing is what is most often heard in Protestant churches in the United States, such as: "The peace of God which passes all understanding keep your hearts and minds in the knowledge and love of God," or, "The Lord bless you and keep you." Another way of closing the service is with an ascription of glory, such as: "And now unto him who is able to keep you from falling . . ." The use of each of these will depend on the season, the theme of the service, and the preference of the minister and congregation. In each case, the final words provide a sense of closure as the congregation leaves worship to serve in Christ's name.

Going Forth. The sense of closure communicated in the benediction may be reinforced by a choral response or congregational "amen." An instrumental postlude may be played as the congregation files out and people turn and greet one another.

Why do these parts of the liturgy come in the *order* they do? Some of it is tradition we have inherited, and traditions vary from one part of the world to another and from one church to another. However, there is a logical, natural progression to events in the service that happen here. A worshiper paying close attention will not be jolted or distracted by what seem to be incongruous or disruptive events in the service.

What Is "Good" Liturgy for Our Church?

Good liturgy articulates the beliefs of the congregation at worship. It is consistent with the faith people claim. It puts into word and act their response to God's goodness, power, and revelation to the world. Good liturgy is honest; it does not make statements that are untruthful about God, the church, or the people who gather there. Good liturgy reflects the values Christians hold because of their faith.

For example, more and more denominations are looking at the language used in their liturgy and hymns, and asking whether it excludes or denigrates people because of race, sex, or nationality. Because they believe God values all persons equally, they do not want their worship to express something contrary to that conviction. Another example of good liturgy is found in the congregation that, out of concern for responsible stewardship of God's creation, does not print a worship bulletin with so many inserts it begins to resemble the Sunday newspaper. Such a church believes that killing trees does not necessarily save souls!

Good liturgy is participatory but not demanding or manipulative. Worship is the work of the people but it is not forced labor. The minister and other worship leaders are reverent but not sanctimonious. They should model what it is that the congregation is being invited to do. Time should be allowed for the congregation to do it. Each worshiper should have the freedom to participate or sit quietly without being made conspicuous. An invitation to come forward for prayer may be a good thing, but not if the minister announces that the service will not end until some poor soul walks down to the front. In like manner, being told during the Peace to look one's neighbor in the eye, hold his or her hand, and sing, "I love you with the love of the Lord," is the liturgical equivalent of ordering a small boy to kiss a relative because it is the relative's birthday. It is not good liturgy, no matter what the denomination.

Good liturgy is clear to regular worshipers and intelligible to visitors. Church members become uneasy and defensive when they cannot figure out things printed in their own Sunday bulletin. One new pastor, for example, put strange notations in the order of service that no one but he could decipher:

Prelude	(church rehearsal)
The Prayer of Confession	(reduce)
Thanksgiving	(God the Father)
The Spirit	(yes)

Because the parenthetical words were an addition to the order of service, worshipers believed the pastor must have thought they were important, but he did not explain their significance. The lay people assumed they had been absent the Sunday the words were "decoded," and the pastor, not being questioned on the matter, may well have assumed the laity understood this addition to the bulletin. The mystery of its meaning was never solved. This example underscores the need for good communication as well as clear, easy to follow bulletins.

Just as congregational resistance to unexplained changes in worship is high, few things daunt a newcomer more than not being able to deduce what happens next, or why. Yet churches continue to print bulletins that might as well be in a foreign language; the needed information is inaccessible to outsiders. An obvious example: page numbers should be given for *every* part of the service in which the worshiper is expected to read, sing, or follow something. Printed rubrics (comments giving directions) should explain what kind of participation is encouraged at various points in the liturgy: standing, kneeling, dipping the bread in the chalice and partaking immediately, and the like. In good liturgy, the Trinity may be an incomprehensible mystery but the order of service is not.

Good liturgy is purposeful activity. It does not occur only because it is eleven o'clock on Sunday morning, but because the things said and done in worship are the congregation's faith-filled response to God. Each act in the liturgy should be a part of that response and a proclamation of what the church's faith is. Go through your church's order of service and ask, "How does each thing listed here worship God and profess the faith we claim? How is it related to whatever comes before and after it?"

A good liturgy facilitates response or evaluation on the part of laity. After a change in the order or style of worship has been implemented, time should be allowed to discuss positive and negative aspects of the change, and the rationale for the change may be reviewed. This serves to remind worshipers of the ground of belief from which their liturgy develops. Specific ways of evaluating aspects of worship are given in the chapter on the role of the laity.

Finally, good liturgy is to the glory of God. It praises the Lord for past mercies and power, acknowledges God's sovereignty, and celebrates God's redemptive act through

Jesus Christ. Good liturgy recognizes the church as God's covenant community, employs the means of grace God established (the sacraments), calls upon the Holy Spirit's wisdom and aid for our endeavors, and proclaims God's Word. Other acts may be done on Sunday morning that are beautiful, family-oriented, enjoyable, consciousness-raising, politically significant, intellectually stimulating or growth enhancing. They are not good liturgy if their primary focus is not the glory of God.

Evaluation of Your Church's Liturgy

Assessing Our Situation

The following questions deal with your understanding of the structure, content, and meaning of your church's liturgy. Please answer these the best you can by making a check in the appropriate place.

1. Does your worship service have what you would call a pattern?

   _____yes   _____uncertain   _____no
2. Is there a logical, smooth flow from one part of the service to the next?

   _____yes   _____uncertain   _____no
3. Does the liturgy reflect and proclaim the beliefs of your congregation and tradition/denomination?

   _____yes   _____uncertain   _____no
4. Can visitors to a worship service understand what is happening?

   _____yes   _____uncertain   _____no
5. Does your church's liturgy teach people as well as inspire them and keep the service orderly?

   _____yes   _____uncertain   _____no
6. Are page numbers listed for every part of the service, where appropriate?

   _____yes   _____uncertain   _____no
7. Are there adequate opportunities for various kinds of participation in the liturgy?

   _____yes   _____uncertain   _____no

8. Do people in the congregation know the source of the materials used in worship?

_____yes   _____uncertain   _____no

9. Do people leading worship communicate reverence and enthusiasm for what they are doing?

_____yes   _____uncertain   _____no

10. Do you believe what you have done in the Sunday morning service is to the glory of God?

_____yes   _____uncertain   _____no

Now go back over your answers to the questions and give each a score. Write the scores in the spaces below. Give each "yes" a score of 3, each "uncertain" a score of 2, and each "no" a score of 1. If you could not answer the question give it a score of 0.

Question	Score
One	_____
Two	_____
Three	_____
Four	_____
Five	_____
Six	_____
Seven	_____
Eight	_____
Nine	_____
Ten	_____
Total	_____

Add the scores. The total may range from 0 (the weakest score) to 30 (the strongest score). How do the scores given by the members of your group compare with each other?

Discussing the Issues

1. To what extent is the liturgy in your church an expression of your faith?

2. Does congregational participation and/or attendance suggest support or lack of support for the church's style of worship?

3. How does your church's liturgy connect you with the person in the next pew, Christians in other traditions, and Christians of other times and places?

4. What was the most talked-about worship service in the last year? Why? What can you learn about liturgy from this?

Responding to the Issues

It has been suggested that all people need ritual in their lives, whether they find it in liturgy or elsewhere, such as in Masonic rites, watching royal pageantry, or maintaining certain family or individual customs. If you accept this statement as true, you may enjoy discussing the similarities and significant differences between these rituals and what happens Sunday morning.

Whether there is intense loyalty to or resistance to the order of service used in your congregation, both point to certain assumptions about the nature of God and about the divine-human relationship. Encouraging conversation about these underlying assumptions may prepare the way for more intentional, participatory, and inviting liturgy in your church.

Notes

Chapter 3

1. James Bulloch, *The Life of the Celtic Church* (Edinburgh: Saint Andrew Press, 1963), p. 208.

2. James F. White, *Introduction to Christian Worship* (Nashville: Abingdon Press, 1980), p. 85.

3. *Ibid.*, p. 86.

Chapter 4

1. J. Gelineau, SJ, "Music and Singing in the Liturgy," in Cheslyn Jones, Geoffrey Wainwright, and Edward Yarnold, *The Study of Liturgy* (New York: Oxford University Press, 1978), p. 441.

2. *Ibid.*, p. 445.

3. White, *Introduction to Christian Worship*, pp. 100–102.

4. *Ibid.*, p. 101.

5. W. J. Hollenweger, "Spirituals," in J. G. Davies, *The New Westminster Dictionary of Liturgy and Worship* (Philadelphia: Westminster Press, 1986), pp. 497–498.

6. Bernarr Rainbow, "Choir (Musical)," in Davies, *The New Westminster Dictionary of Liturgy and Worship*, p. 165.

7. Franky Schaeffer, *Addicted to Mediocrity* (Westchester, Illinois: Crossway Books, 1981).

Chapter 5

1. William D. Thompson, *Preaching Biblically: Exegesis and Interpretation* (Nashville: Abingdon Press, 1981), p. 7.

2. Conrad Massa, "Preaching as Confluence" (inaugural address), *The Princeton Seminary Bulletin*, vol. 1, no. 3 (new series, 1979).

Chapter 6

1. R. C. D. Jasper, "Liturgies," in Davies, *The New Westminster Dictionary of Liturgy and Worship*, p. 314.

2. *The United Methodist Hymnal* (Nashville: The United Methodist Publishing House, 1989), p. 3.

3. Peter G. Cobb, "The Liturgy of the Word in the Early Church," in Jones, Wainwright, and Yarnold, *The Study of Liturgy*, p. 182.

4. E. C. Ratcliff, "The Choir Offices: The Litany," in W. K. Lowther Clarke, ed., *Liturgy and Worship* (1932), pp. 282–287 (quoted in W. Jardine Grisbrooke, "Litany," in Davies, *The New Westminster Dictionary of Liturgy and Worship*, p. 305).

For Further Reading

J. D. Crichton. *Christian Celebration: The Mass.* London: Geoffrey Chapman, 1971.

Kendig Brubaker Cully, ed. *Confirmation: History/Doctrine and Practice.* Greenwich, Conn.: Seabury Press, 1962.

J. G. Davies, ed. *The New Westminster Dictionary of Liturgy and Worship.* Philadelphia: Westminster Press, 1986.

Hoyt L. Hickman. *A Primer for Church Worship.* Nashville: Abingdon Press, 1984.

Richard Lischer. *Theories of Preaching.* Durham, N. C.: Labyrinth Press, 1987.

Thomas G. Long. *The Senses of Preaching.* Atlanta: John Knox Press, 1988.

Donald Macleod. *Presbyterian Worship: Its Meaning and Method.* Atlanta: John Knox Press, 1980.

Bard Thompson. *Liturgies of the Western Church.* Cleveland: Collins, 1961.

Max Thurian and Geoffrey Wainwright, eds. *Baptism and Eucharist: Ecumenical Convergence in Celebration.* Geneva: World Council of Churches, and Grand Rapids, Mich.: Wm. B. Eerdmans Publishing Co., 1983.

James F. White, *Introduction to Christian Worship.* Nashville: Abingdon Press, 1980.

Index